Comments on other *Amazing Stories* from readers & reviewers

"You might call them the non-fiction response to Harlequin romances: easy to consume and potentially addictive."
Robert Martin, *The Chronicle Herald*

"Tightly written volumes filled with lots of wit and humour about famous and infamous Canadians."
Eric Shackleton, *The Globe and Mail*

"This is popular history as it should be... For this price, buy two and give one to a friend."
Terry Cook, a reader from Ottawa, on **Rebel Women**

"Stories are rich in description, and bristle with a clever, stylish realness."
Mark Weber, *Central Alberta Advisor*, on **Ghost Town Stories II**

"The resulting book is one readers will want to share with all the women in their lives."
Lynn Martel, *Rocky Mountain Outlook*, on **Women Explorers**

"[The books are] *long on plot and character and short on the sort of technical analysis that can be dreary for all but the most committed academic."*
Robert Martin, *The Chronicle Herald*

"A compelling read. Bertin ... has selected only the most intriguing tales, which she narrates with a wealth of detail."
Joyce Glasner, *New Brunswick Reader*, on **Strange Events**

"The heightened sense of drama and intrigue, combined with a good dose of human interest is what sets Amazing Stories *apart."*
Pamela Klaffke, *Calgary Herald*

INSPIRING
ANIMAL TALES

AMAZING STORIES®

INSPIRING ANIMAL TALES

Heartwarming Stories of
Courage and Devotion

by Roxanne Willems Snopek

PUBLISHED BY ALTITUDE PUBLISHING CANADA LTD.
1500 Railway Avenue, Canmore, Alberta T1W 1P6
www.altitudepublishing.com
www.amazingstories.ca
1-800-957-6888

Extreme care has been taken to ensure that all information presented in
this book is accurate and up to date. Neither the author nor the
publisher can be held responsible for any errors.

Publisher	Stephen Hutchings
Associate Publisher	Kara Turner
Editor	Deborah Lawson
Cover and Layout	Bryan Pezzi

We acknowledge the financial support of the Government
of Canada through the Book Publishing Industry Development
Program (BPIDP) for our publishing activities.

Altitude GreenTree Program
Altitude Publishing will plant twice as many trees as were used
in the manufacturing of this product.

Library and Archives Canada Cataloguing in Publication

Snopek, Roxanne Willems
  Inspiring animal tales / Roxanne Willems Snopek.

(Amazing stories)
ISBN 1-55439-047-8

  1. Human-animal relationships--Anecdotes. 2. Animals--Anecdotes.
I. Title. II. Series: Amazing stories (Canmore, Alta.)

QL791.S66 2005   590   C2005-905747-5i

Amazing Stories® is a registered trademark of Altitude Publishing Canada Ltd.

Printed and bound in Canada by Friesens
2 4 6 8 9 7 5 3

In memory of Simon and Cody,
our Ontario cats.

Contents

Prologue

Summer heat hung languid in the air. On the beach at Port Dover, parents sprawled on colourful chairs fanning themselves, while their children waded out as far as possible into the shallow lake. At the food stand, the vendor hustled to keep up with non-stop orders for soft drinks, foot-long hot dogs, and French fries.

Tim and Trish Brown arranged their family at the picnic table and set out their meal. Hot and hungry, everyone needed to eat, especially their autistic son, Matthew. Whenever they go out with their son, the Browns are on high alert. They sat him securely between them on the bench, but he wasn't happy. His agitation increased until they knew they had no choice but to pack up and go home as quickly as possible. Tim and Trish scrambled to gather their things, juggling picnic baskets and bags of wet towels while making sure someone always had a firm hand on Matthew. Like many people with autism, Matthew is completely unable to grasp the concept of danger. Through the crowded parking lot, each of them gripped one of his hands.

Suddenly he wriggled free and bolted, heedless of traffic. Both parents shrieked and ran after him, but Matthew, who loves nothing better than being chased, had the edge. Other times when he'd gotten away from them, they'd been able to catch up with him in time to prevent disaster.

But this time they were in a parking lot swarming with impatient drivers. Worse yet, the parking lot exited onto a high-traffic main road. This appeared to be Matthew's goal.

Tim ran, hoping against hope that he might overtake the energetic youngster. Terror spurred his feet; he knew that if he couldn't catch up, his son would sprint straight into several lanes of traffic going in both directions.

The distance between them was narrow, but Matthew had too much of a head start. If he reached the road, the results would almost certainly be tragic. There wasn't time to think, but in the slow-motion horror of the moment, Tim prepared himself for the worst. "Even with my adrenaline pumping and running as fast as I could," recalls Tim, "I was unable to catch him."

Suddenly a car just ahead of Matthew nosed cautiously into his pathway. Confused, he slowed his pace. Within moments, Tim reached him. "An alert motorist had seen the look of horror on my husband's face and blocked the exit with her car," explains Trish. "This prevented Matt from running into the roadway, and gave my husband enough time to catch up and restrain him."

Once the dust settled and their heart rates returned to normal, Tim and Trish looked at one another, each knowing exactly what the other was thinking. This simply must not happen again, ever. They'd heard about service dogs for autis-

Prologue

tic kids, but hadn't decided whether or not a dog would be the answer. Now they knew they had to give it a try. Things couldn't get worse.

Chapter 1
Full Partner, For Life

At 2 a.m. the streets of Guelph were silent, dark, and empty. Well, almost empty. On both sides, up and down the avenue, houses were locked up tightly, the curtains were pulled, and residents lay asleep in their beds, secure in their homes, not realizing their sense of safety was only an illusion. That night in the quiet neighbourhood, a stealthy lurker checked house after house, trying to gain entrance without awakening the occupants. Finally, he found a good prospect. Inside, an old woman dozed in front of the television, never imagining that at her back door crouched a desperate intruder, picking the lock with frantic fingers.

He glanced over his shoulder. The neighbourhood may have been sleeping, but a prickly heat on the back of his neck made him feel he was being watched, as though someone was after him. Maybe the stalker was being stalked. Suddenly he heard the soft crunch of feet on snow. He knew his pursuers were near. He had become the prey. Recklessly he worked the doorknob, and a moment later the tumblers fell into place. He pushed open the door, tiptoed in, and hunkered down, waiting for the hunters to pass. The woman inside, incredibly, continued to sleep.

An hour earlier and a few houses away, hunger had sent another neighbourhood resident ambling into the kitchen looking for a snack. His mind was focused on his stomach; did he want peanut butter and jelly, or leftover pizza? When he turned on the light, it took him a moment to process the fact that a strange man stood in his kitchen. But in that split second, he knew he had to take action. He yelled and the stranger fled into the night. With shaking fingers, he dialled the police station. "I just chased an intruder out of my house!"

Constable Dave Guest and police service dog Nero arrived on the scene within minutes. Dave listened to the frightened man's story. Because the resident hadn't heard the sound of a vehicle, the suspect was probably on foot. Dave thought it likely that the intruder was still hiding in the vicinity, perhaps waiting to break into another home. "Search!" he instructed Nero. Immediately the dog went to work. Keeping a tight hold on the leash, Dave followed just behind Nero's waving tail. The dog was completely focused, sniffing from side to side, straining to go faster. He paused. Which way? He lifted his head to scent the air. Back and forth he tested the wind, nostrils flaring delicately. Then his sophisticated olfactory organ caught the elusive scent molecules of his prey and he leaped back into the chase.

Nero's excitement pointed towards a very fresh trail. "He must be nearby," thought Dave. The dog dove into a patch of rough bush. Dave followed, shielding his face from whipping branches that scratched his skin. The dog had no such concerns and barrelled on ahead, into the backyard and around the fence of the next home. For over an hour they searched in this fashion, up one walkway, down another. "I thought I was following the postman," says Dave. He might have doubted the wisdom of their task, if it weren't for Nero. "When the scent gets stronger, Nero pulls harder and his tail wags more, so I knew we were right there," says Dave.

Clearly, the dog knew the suspect was only steps ahead. Every muscle in his body quivered with the thrill of the hunt and the anticipation of success. Suddenly, at the back of yet another house, his tail went up. He leaped up the steps to the backdoor and began barking. Dave knew their search was over; through the glass in the patio door he could see the suspect. Before Dave had to do anything, the would-be thief stepped out with his hands up, palms open. Nero's bark had been enough. The terrified man was taking no chances. He flattened himself on the ground, and held out his wrists. "We found him hiding inside the back door of a house where an elderly lady was asleep on the couch, just feet away from the door," says Dave. "We started tracking at 2 a.m. We arrested him at 3:40."

Inside the house the woman woke from her sleep, but by the time she reached the door it was all over. Thanks to Dave and Nero, the intruder was captured before he could do any more harm.

It was just another night on the job for Nero. And for his good work, he got a reward: a moment to play with his favourite rubber Kong® toy. That, and the praise of Dave, his partner and master, is all he wants out of life.

In 1998, when the Guelph Police Service decided to add a canine unit, Nero was their first dog. A purebred German shepherd, from champion Czechoslovakian bloodlines, Nero initially trained with the Toronto Police Service in their 16-week basic canine-handlers course. Then he joined the Guelph force as a general-purpose patrol dog and a partner for Dave. In addition to tracking, Nero is trained in obedience, agility, article/evidence search, and apprehension. Like all police service dogs, Nero is highly responsive to his handler and under iron-clad control. A single word from Dave is all it takes to command Nero.

If a suspect threatens Dave, tries to escape, or starts fighting, Nero won't hesitate to use his formidable strength to restrain the aggressor. His presence alone is often sufficient to make suspects think twice about arguing. One call led the team to the home of an elderly man who had been savagely

Dave Guest and Nero

beaten in a mafia-style attack. Just as they arrived, two suspects ran from the house. The officers quickly established a perimeter to prevent them from leaving the area, but because the suspects were armed they waited to arrest them until members of the tactical team arrived. The direction of the wind was perfect to bring the scent straight to them, and from Nero's excitement, Dave knew he was picking up some strong signals. "Nero kept looking to the backyard, so I knew there was a suspect somewhere around there," recalls Dave. As soon as the other officers arrived, Dave gave Nero his head. "A man was hiding behind a garden shed," he says. "The guy had a knife, but as soon as Nero came at him, barking, he put up his hands and complied." The perpetrator knew he'd been caught, fair and square.

Nero also has an amazing ability to assess a situation, often leaping to Dave's aid before Dave even knows he needs it. When a local donut shop was robbed, police were alarmed to learn that the suspect claimed to have a bomb in his duffle bag. Officers had located him, chased him around a number of commercial buildings, and had almost caught him when Nero and Dave arrived. "I jumped out of the cruiser to assist one of the officers," he relates. "As we were struggling with the suspect, Nero also jumped out the cruiser window and assisted in subduing the man." As soon as Nero came on the scene the suspect stopped fighting. Dave then called off the dog. Nero backed down instantly; he'd accomplished what he intended to. "He saw me working and jumped out to help me.

I hadn't told him to, hadn't expected him to, but he was going to be involved in the action with me. When I reacted," says Dave, "he reacted, too, based on my actions."

Nero-as-backup is an image not soon forgotten. With habitual criminals, this police dog has attained an almost mythical status. One man, detained by another canine unit, said to the arresting officer, "Good thing it's not Nero; he's arrested me twice before!"

And yet, in Nero's long career, not once has he seriously injured a suspect. When one offender, previously arrested by Nero, found himself in trouble again, it was obvious he wasn't nearly as worried about going back to prison as he was about possibly meeting his canine nemesis. "I didn't like that dog," he told the officer who brought him in. Then he pulled up his sleeve to show two tiny scratches, the only marks remaining from teeth that could have torn his arm apart. "He's not a weapon," says Dave. "He's a locating tool."

This tool has proved invaluable time and time again. The city of Guelph has a mobile library — a bookmobile — that travels about, allowing access to people that might otherwise be unable to use the library. Between travels, this converted motor home is parked beside one of the regional library branches. One night hoodlums broke into the bookmobile and set it ablaze. Before long, it exploded.

"Nero and I tracked from the scene, locating several discarded books and magazines along the way," says Dave. The litter of books and paper led from the bookmobile to an adjacent park and up a walkway until, abruptly, the track disappeared. There were no more books or papers — and no scent. To Dave's dismay, it started to rain. Even though the scent would be harder for Nero to find, they continued. They followed the curving street around until it reconnected with the library and bookmobile site. Dave watched Nero for any sign of hope. There it was! Nero's tail went up, indicating he'd detected the scent again. This time he ignored the walkway that had led to the dead end, and proceeded to a backyard nearby. "Nero was all over this garden shed, walking around it, holding up his tail. We checked, but there was no one in it." Dave was mystified, but he knew they were close.

Nero's tracking gave officers sufficient grounds to awaken the homeowner for questioning, but the man insisted everyone in the house was present and accounted for. So Dave and Nero went back to the shed for a closer look. This time they hit pay dirt. Tucked inside, they found books, a first-aid kit, a calculator, a flashlight, and other items, all clearly identified as belonging to the bookmobile. When Dave and Nero paid another visit to the house, the father admitted that his son and two of his friends had been out during the night. "That gave us grounds to arrest them, or at least detain them," says Dave. "When we took them in, they confessed."

The kids boasted to the detectives that they'd deliberately tossed books up the walkway to misguide the dog. "It's due to a little luck and a little experience that Nero was able to relocate the scent and follow it successfully," says Dave. "A less experienced dog might not have been able to do it."

Dave is quick to give credit to the teamwork of his platoon. "I have to say that for all these calls, the dog helps, but the other officers have already set the scene and established the perimeter." When Dave and Nero are called in to a situation, they're given a description of the suspect and the direction he's travelling. Without this information, they'd have a tough time. "You're only as good as the other officers supporting you," Dave emphasizes. "Nero's success is our whole platoon's success."

Some nights, things don't work out. It's discouraging, but canine handlers know it's just a matter of time until they nab their next one. On the shift he's most proud of, Dave and Nero helped arrest an astounding eight people in a single night.

The evening began with a call to track two kids who'd been seen breaking into cars. They'd eluded the officer chasing them, but Nero tracked them through a townhouse complex to a neighbouring backyard. Meanwhile, another officer was heading over from a different part of the city to assist them. When he turned on his roof lights to clear the road, a van in front of him, instead of pulling over, sped up, jerking erratically from side to side. The officer gave chase and eventually the van crashed. Five people leaped out and took off. "By this time," remembers Dave, "all the officers that were coming to help *me* ended up going to help this other officer instead — including Nero and me!" Nero and Dave hit the ground running, and quickly located all five people hiding in a bush next to the side of a house. The group turned out to be a break-and-enter team, on its way to rob a local business.

A few hours later, at 4 a.m., they were called to a break-in at a gas bar where the suspect had stolen cigarettes. "We tracked him for about two-and-a-half kilometres through freezing rain and could see he was heading downtown. Another officer saw the suspect standing outside a homeless shelter and recognized him from the security camera photo," says Dave. With an officer on one side and Nero and Dave on the other, the thief knew there was no point in running anymore. "You're on top of the world when you find somebody," Dave says. "When you find lots of people, your dog is the greatest."

Nero and Dave have an impressive athletic record as well, placing first overall, twice in their region, at the United States Police Canine Association Police Dog 1 Trials. In those same trials in Florida, they finished 18th overall nationally, out of 162 teams. The pair also finished third overall out of 65 teams in the Virginia "Iron Dog" competition, a 5.6 km obstacle course through the state's beautiful mountains.

Nero was scheduled to work until the end of 2004, but in May of that year, while tracking a commercial break-and-enter suspect, he ruptured a disc in his neck jumping down from a retaining wall. He recovered from the injury, but the incident reminded everyone that working dogs aren't invincible and that Nero isn't a young dog anymore. Rather than risk more serious injuries, Nero was given early retirement. He continues to live with Dave but no longer accompanies him to work, a difficult adjustment for both of them.

During the seven years Nero and Dave worked together, they were involved in 733 calls for service and assisted in more than 200 criminal arrests. They also participated in over 100 community demonstrations to raise public awareness of the work of police service dogs and to thank their supporters.

Police work creates strong bonds between team members. They seldom think of the risks they face each day, but nevertheless, they know every call they attend could be the one that ends in tragedy. Partners protect each other, and Nero was as trustworthy as any human partner. "After Nero retired we were called to a gas station robbery where a guy had a gun." Dave positioned his patrol car to obstruct what he expected would be the suspect's escape route. Just as he expected, the thief burst onto the street, riding his bike straight towards him. As soon as he saw Dave, he changed direction, taking off into a wooded area. "I ran after him, but stopped at a fence and thought 'This guy is supposed to be armed. What am I doing?' That's when I realized I'm in a different job now. I don't have Nero, my security blanket and guardian angel, with me anymore."

Fellow officers understand how much Dave misses his partner. They all know that losing a trusted partner, even to retirement, is difficult. "When I first went back out without

Nero, they gave me a picture of him in a plastic frame to take with me in my car," says Dave.

And when Constable Dave Guest goes home at the end of the day, Nero's exuberant welcome is the first thing to greet him. The waving tail, the nuzzling and leaning — all remind Dave that even though his old partner no longer fights crime with him, there's no doubt he'd still lay down his life without hesitation for the man he loves.

Chapter 2
When Wishes
Are Horses

ind streaming through her hair, the earth rushing past beneath her, the rhythmic sound of pounding hoof beats — these were Jenni Rowe's idea of heaven. Animals of every kind had always fascinated her, but horses were her special love. To be around them, she cleaned barns for friends, opened and closed gates, helped catch reluctant mounts, fetched and carried tack, and hauled grain and hay. One gallop through a field, sharing the joy of movement and speed with her favourite animals, made it all worthwhile.

In February of 1994, an encounter with high speed changed Jenni's life disastrously. She and two of her friends were driving through the darkness of a frigid winter night. In a split second, their laughter and excitement turned to terror, as headlights that should have passed them by swerved over the centre line with deadly speed. Jenni and her friends braced themselves, powerless to avoid the maelstrom around them. Tires screamed. Metal shrieked against metal. Glass exploded.

Until the wailing of voices and sirens began, the air was deathly silent. From the pick-up truck that had hit them, there was neither movement nor sound; it had been going so fast that when they collided, the truck flipped right over their car. The driver had been killed instantly. They would learn later that he had a blood alcohol level of 0.316 percent, almost four times the legal limit. Worse yet, he had a long history of impaired driving.

When the wreckage of the collision settled, Jenni's friends were battered and bruised but they would be okay. Jenni, however, lay unconscious — crushed and bleeding in the twisted automobile. She was 16 years old.

The list of Jenni's injuries included damaged nerves, a fracture at the third lumbar vertebra, and a spinal cord injury at the third thoracic vertebra, where a blood vessel had ruptured. She had a broken ankle, three broken ribs, a ruptured bowel and a lacerated liver. Doctors were blunt. "Your spinal cord is severed," they told her. "You'll never walk again." As Jenni recalls, "The surgeon and doctors actually said they had never seen an injury like mine before."

Chest-level spinal cord injuries can result in quadriplegia. Until more time passed, no one knew if this would be her fate. As Jenni lay in her bed, floating in and out of consciousness, she didn't think about riding. She didn't think about walking. What she did think about, wonder about, was whether or not she'd ever be able to do anything, even something as simple as sitting up, by herself. After three weeks in the hospital she was discharged. They'd patched her up as best they could.

"I was admitted to a rehabilitation facility," says Jenni, "where they were trying to get me adjusted to life in a wheelchair. They wanted to get me as independent as possible." A multitude of caregivers worked with her during those weeks: a psychologist, a social worker, a recreational therapist, an occupational therapist, and of course, the physiotherapist. "I'd always been on a swim team growing up, so I loved the pool," says Jenni. She spent hours there, relearning how to use her body, coaxing, prodding, and begging her muscles for just the slightest movement. It was hard work, with little to show for it except fatigue and discouragement.

Then Jenni had a dream. Beside her hospital bed stood a horse she'd loved as a child. She saw herself seated on the horse. This vision of herself — out of bed and mounted again on a horse — galvanized Jenni's hope. The horse symbolized freedom and mobility, an opportunity to go places not accessible by wheelchair. "I realized that if I was able to get on a horse, the horse would be my legs," she recalls.

Jenni refused to allow herself unrealistic hopes. She'd seen people in denial go to incredible expense and effort, only to be forced, ultimately, to face a lifetime without walking. "I decided to get on with my life in a wheelchair," she says. "I wasn't surrendering to it; I was accepting it." She imagined her entire future in a wheelchair: going to her prom, getting married, having children, all in a wheelchair. Her life had been indisputably *changed*, but she was determined it would not be *destroyed*.

On her grandmother's birthday, Jenni made an astonishing discovery. She could wiggle her toe! "I was excited but my doctor said, 'You can't walk on a toe.' I figured any movement was better than nothing. If that was all I was going to get, I'd enjoy it. I'd appreciate that toe."

Jenni continued working with the rehabilitation team for two and a half months and slowly regained a bit more movement. Then she was sent home. "After I got home and started exercising in my parents' pool, a whole bunch of movement came back," she remembers. At her next regular physiotherapy appointment, the therapist suggested she put on leg braces and try standing. Not only could she stand up, she even managed a couple of steps.

The doctors had been wrong. Her badly damaged spinal cord had *not* been completely severed. There *was* a chance she would walk again. Jenni was fitted for long leg braces — moulded prosthetic devices that fit snugly from hip to foot, allowing the wearer to walk by throwing the leg forward from the hip. It took two months to make the braces, and in that time Jenni directed all her efforts towards strengthening the necessary muscles. The braces arrived in September 1994, just in time for her return to school.

Six months later she switched to short braces, supports that extend from just below the knee to under the foot, but these didn't last long either. "One night I got up — again on my grandmother's birthday — and didn't bother to put on the braces. I ended up falling and broke my toe. Of course, it swelled up and until it healed I couldn't use the braces. I had to manage without them and found out I could!" Jenni attended her high-school graduation ceremony, not in a wheelchair as she'd imagined, not with leg braces, but on her own two feet.

Few things are more difficult for a teenager than standing out from the crowd and Jenni had to face the fact that some of her friends couldn't cope with her injury. Her physical appearance had changed. Mentally and emotionally, she was dealing with issues far greater than most of them would ever face. Even something as small as spontaneous outings separated her from her peers. "It was difficult for me to get around because everything had to be planned, and that's not something teens really understand," Jenni says.

She was mobile once again but now what? Jenni decided to continue pursuing her goal of becoming a zoologist and was accepted at the University of Guelph. "I'd always been fascinated by Dian Fossey and Jane Goodall," says Jenni. "All I had ever wanted to do was be a field researcher, studying things like conservation and animal behaviour."

But she never forgot the dream she'd had in the hospital. Jenni missed the pungent aroma of the stables, the snorts and whinnies of excitement, the sense of human-equine partnership. She decided to try horse-back riding again. "I started taking riding lessons once a week."

It was a bittersweet pleasure; she came home from her first lesson feeling completely defeated. "This stable had never worked with a disabled rider before, so it was a bit nerve-wracking. I had someone on each side of me, one holding my legs, another person holding the reins, and it was still everything I could do just to stay in the saddle." Perhaps her vision of galloping over the fields with wind rushing through her hair would never come to pass. But she kept on, hoping things would improve.

She finished her first year in zoology, and began summer work with one of her professors. "One day we went out to do some field research, and we had to go down a hill to a stream," Jenni says. "Going down the hill wasn't difficult for anyone else, but they had to carry me down and sit me in a chair." After that day, Jenni had to face the fact that she'd be able to work in a laboratory, but not as a field researcher. She switched her course of study to psychology. "It was probably the hardest decision I'd made in my life."

Reality set in with a vengeance, and Jenni's optimism was severely shaken. She couldn't have the career she'd always wanted. Her physical recovery had reached a plateau. She couldn't ride like she used to. Frustrated, she decided she might do better at a different riding centre. Getting out her phone book, she discovered the Canadian Therapeutic Riding Association and the sport of dressage.

"That's where everything took off for me," she says. "I didn't know anything about dressage until then, but I fell in love with it." Dressage involves guiding a horse through a series of complex manoeuvres using only subtle movements of hands and legs and slight shifts of weight. It requires tremendous muscle control. A related form of dressage is the musical *kur* or freestyle ride, composed of one, two, or more horses, performing to music. In the kur rides, sport becomes art, a magical dance where horse and rider seem to become one. "When done correctly, the horse and rider are engaged in an intricate dance, each — with no visible signs — anticipating and responding to the other's moves," says Jenni. "It looks like the riders are sitting motionless as the horses dance beneath them." To see riders with disabilities participating in such a beautiful and challenging sport was a revelation.

Jenni was put on a male chestnut quarter horse named Chelsea. With the expert training and assistance she received, Jenni re-learned to ride. Soon she was riding two or three times each week. She'll never forget the first time she cantered unassisted. "Chelsea's the most dependable horse and I knew he wouldn't put a foot out of place, so I felt very safe."

It couldn't have come at a better time for Jenni. The nerve damage resulting from her injury had begun to cause episodes of severe pain that, many nights, kept her awake until dawn. It started with hot poker-like sensations shooting down the fronts of her legs. The sensations intensified for about five seconds, then faded, only to begin again moments later. "Unfortunately, my pain is the worst when my muscles are relaxed," says Jenni. "Something about muscles flexing around the nerves seem to quiet them. This means my pain hits most when I'm sitting in a car or a plane, and especially when I'm trying to sleep. When it's really bad, I pace the floors in a stupor, hardly able to hold myself up."

Between her constant pain and the ostracism Jenni faced at university, her self-confidence could not have sunk lower. Riding gave her something to hold on to. "Horses don't care what you look like, or if you walk funny and don't conform to the norm," says Jenni. "Horses were there for me when I felt like I had no one else. They never turned away. They were a warm body to be close to, a soft touch, a warm nuzzle on the shoulder, a long mane to cry into, broad shoulders to carry a load too heavy to manage on my own."

She struggled to keep up with her classes, but she was so sleep-deprived that she decided not to return for the second semester. As spring neared, her pain abated somewhat. "I kept riding at the centre, mostly on Chelsea," Jenni says. "I was becoming more and more focused on dressage, working to improve my performance. It was a great stress reliever."

Whether Jenni realized it or not, Chelsea was doing far more than relieving her stress. Therapeutic riding, also known as hippo-therapy or equine facilitated therapy, is a well-recognized rehabilitative activity. Riding was first used for this purpose around the turn of the century and by the 1950s British physiotherapists were exploring the use of riding therapy for all types of handicaps. In 1969, The North American Riding for the Handicapped Association (NARHA) was founded to provide safety guidelines, instructor training and certification, and accreditation for facilities.

People with many different types of disabilities respond to equestrian therapy, but for those with mobility problems resulting from such things as spina bifida, cerebral palsy, or spinal cord injuries, it works a special magic. Sitting astride a horse's back challenges tight leg and back muscles, while the warmth of the animal underneath gently stretches them and increases their flexibility. Balancing on the horse stimulates the muscles and nerves in the head, neck, and trunk, helping riders develop greater midline control, improving their posture and muscle tone. But perhaps the best thing about riding therapy is the growth in self-confidence. Simply being up high, in control of a large, powerful animal, is tremendously affirming, something Jenni needed desperately just then. Chelsea gave that to her.

That summer Jenni decided to try competing. "Chelsea and I went in a show, a provincial competition against other disabled riders," she says. "We got the high point score of the day and ended up with a really nice plaque to hang on the wall for the year." The plaque was engraved with names of past winners, many of whom had gone on to become international competitors. Suddenly, Jenni saw riding in a different light.

Ever since the 1969 Paralympic Games first included equestrian events, in Atlanta, Georgia, dressage for disabled riders has grown in popularity. Competitors are judged on their horsemanship skills as they ride, using a series of commands for walk, trot, and canter. Riders may use permitted compensating aids such as dressage whips, a connecting rein bar, rubber bands, or other aids.

Although Jenni still needed help with things like getting her horse in from the field, she no longer needed riding "therapy"; what she needed to take her skill to the next level was an actual dressage trainer — and a horse of her own. "I went to a national competition in British Columbia and met Copper Rose," says Jenni. An eye-catching chestnut thoroughbred, Rose also proved to be sweet, dependable, and talented, exactly the type of horse Jenni needed.

For the next year and a half, with Rose, Jenni's ability blossomed. They competed regularly, and before she knew it they were ready for even bigger challenges. Jenni urged Rose towards the more complicated moves but found, to her dismay, that Rose had reached the limit of her abilities. The truth was unavoidable: in order to take her sport to the next level, she'd have to get a different horse. But how could she say good-bye to Rose? "It's hard when you're serious about competing," Jenni admits, "because you have to be willing to move on when the time comes. You're not supposed to be sentimental."

As luck would have it, an elegant solution was just around the corner. "Another Paralympic competitor was riding a horse named Lucy at the time," says Jenni. "He was more disabled than I am, and found that Lucy's movement was too much for him." She suggested he try riding Rose and she would try Lucy. "In the end, we swapped horses," she says. "It's perfect, because we're friends and we knew each of us could see our old horses at competitions."

Equestrian events such as dressage emphasize the partnership of the horse and rider; the pair should function as a unit, rather than the horse mechanically obeying the rider's instructions. Since Jenni had enjoyed such a special relationship with Rose, she didn't expect more than a business-like, working relationship with this new horse. But Lucy surprised her. "I've developed a bond with Lucy like I've had with no other horse," says Jenni. "She's so dependable." Jenni uses a large mounting block, something many horses are uncomfortable with. But instead of walking away before she's fully settled in the saddle, Lucy allows Jenni to use her body for support, standing steadily until she knows her rider is safely up and ready to go. She seems to understand Jenni's limitations, too. "I fall down all the time," Jenni adds. "But even when I fall right under her feet, she just stands there and waits for me to get up."

Chelsea, Copper Rose, and Lucy have carried Jenni

to successes that would hardly be believable if not for the trophies and ribbons lining her walls. In the Paralympic qualifier, the Canadian Open, Jenni won in all classes and was named reserve champion of the entire competition. At the Detroit Dressage Show, another Paralympic qualifier for American and Canadian competitors, she won two firsts and a second and was named grand champion of the entire event. She won the Inner Vision Dressage championship, and has competed on the Paralympic Dressage team at the World Championships in Belgium, as well as the European Dressage Championship in Portugal. "I competed at two qualifiers this year on Lucy," says Jenni, "and it's the greatest feeling. You go into the ring knowing she is going to put every single foot in the right place. She's working so hard and she's doing it totally for you. That's what I really love about it: the mastery of the sport and the bond with the horse. The winning is just gravy."

But in the glory of winning Jenni never forgets her dream, how all she yearned for was to be on a horse again, riding through a field, just the two of them. "The most amazing thing for me is just being able to ride her every day," says Jenni. "Competing internationally has always been important, but the exciting and important things for me are the journey now, not the destination. It's the everyday things with Lucy that I treasure."

Today Jenni continues riding, although she has scaled it back somewhat. She is now married and has completed her studies at the University of Guelph. "It took me seven years, including three summer semesters, to complete my degree," she says, "but I'm planning to return to grad school to do a Masters of Social Work. I know there will be challenges but I want to counsel others who have gone through traumatic accidents or experiences, or people who deal with chronic pain."

Lucy, now 14, probably has another four years of competition left. Regardless of her schedule, Jenni makes sure her beloved horse stays in top form. "It's good for horses to keep working as they age," she says. "I can't imagine selling her, even when she can't do dressage anymore. I want to keep her forever, because she's given me so much."

The past decade has brought changes beyond what Jenni could have ever imagined, from utter despair to hope, from failure to dizzying success. "I refuse to call what happened to me an accident," says Jenni. "It was a crash. It was predictable and preventable." She has spent a great deal of time and energy dealing with the effects of impaired driving on her life. "Nine months after the crash I started speaking to teens about impaired driving, about what happened to me, the consequences, and how it can be prevented," she says. In addition to her equestrian travelling, Jenni has toured the country speaking to conferences, high schools, universities, police colleges, and impaired driving offenders. A video of her story, entitled "Every Day After," was filmed in 2000 and made available to all high schools across the country. "This work has been so meaningful to me, as I know I have saved other lives across Canada," she says.

For Jenni, horses have been the key to her recovery. "They taught me to not necessarily believe something will always be impossible, just because it might look impossible at one point," she concludes. "There are so many twists and turns in life."

Chapter 3
A Babysitter
Named King

The woodland meadow outside Picton in Ontario's beautiful Prince Edward County is a favourite place for picnickers. Under blue skies they lie on blankets, sipping icy drinks on lazy summer afternoons. On sweltering weekends drivers scramble for parking spots and the air fills with the sounds of people relaxing in the heat. Laughter and the shrieks of children mingle with the noise of barking dogs and burgers sizzling over coal fires. It's like any other regional park — except for one thing. Now and then the mothers stop spreading sunblock and children pause in their games. They look up, their eyes wide. They've just heard something they won't hear at any other park. They've heard the unmistakable roar of a lion.

A Babysitter Named King

Their ears aren't playing tricks on them; there *are* lions nearby. Pat and Joe Bergeron live with their family of animals on a small and unusual hobby farm nearby, named the Bergeron Exotic Animal Sanctuary. Pat and Joe have always been animal lovers. German shepherd dogs follow them around, cats perch on every countertop, and goats and chickens peer from the outbuildings. It's the cats that really appeal to them, though. And not just any cats. The Bergerons like *big* cats, and 17 years ago, they decided to get a cougar. "It started with us wanting to own just one," says Pat.

Their research revealed both good and bad news. The good news was that they were already well-equipped to keep such an animal. They had plenty of experience with a variety of animals and their home was private and spacious. The bad news was that no one seemed to care whether or not they would make good owners. "It was disturbing to see how many big cats were out there, and how easy it was to get one," says Pat. Even with all their prior knowledge, they felt they had much to learn; how could all these animals possibly be receiving adequate care?

They suspected many weren't. All they could do was make sure *their* cougar, a female named Casey, had the best life possible. She came from a zoo as a young cub and spent her first year with them in the house. "Casey's such a good cat," says Pat fondly. One cat often leads to another, however, and when the same zoo called to say they had three newborn cougar cubs needing homes, Pat and Joe quickly agreed to

One of the Bergerons' cougars

take one, a male they named Axel. They were delighted to have a companion for Casey, who'd grown too large to live in the house full-time. They hoped Axel would keep Casey from being lonely in her outdoor enclosure. Not only did Casey approve, it was love at first sight.

Within a few years, the Bergerons had added even more cats: a jaguar; a pair of African lions; and another "house-cat," a Siberian tiger. King and Shadow, their German shepherd dogs, saw nothing unusual about this. At mealtimes they waited impatiently while Pat dished up at the various feeding stations. Beside them stood an animal that could have ripped them to shreds if he'd wanted to, but to them, this Siberian tiger was just another roommate.

It's just as well they hold this attitude, for in Pat's world, one is the loneliest number. "I started to raise another tiger cub as company for the one we had," she says. "I had the baby in the house so I could bottle-feed it."

Hand-raising baby mammals — domestic or wild — is a daunting responsibility. The foster parent must take over every single task the mother would normally do. After each feeding, for instance, the mother licks the babies from one end to the other. This stimulates the infants to eliminate and, naturally, the mother cleans it up. So after giving her tiger cub its bottle, Pat took out the paper towelling and massaged and stroked its little bottom. The German shepherd, King, watched with great interest. He hovered so closely, in fact, that he got in the way! "He was such a nuisance, licking them, that I'd have to push him away," says Pat. "Then I realized that he was actually trying to help!" King wasn't just nuzzling and licking the baby tiger; he was actually cleaning up after it, just like its mother would. "So that became our routine," says Pat. "I'd feed the baby and he'd wait beside me until the baby was finished the bottle. It was a lot neater than me using a roll of paper towels!"

Each time a new baby arrived at their home, King was as excited as Pat. Whenever Pat settled down on the couch with a cub snug and secure in her arms, King sat at her feet, anxiously awaiting his turn. "I had to tell him, 'No, no, wait till the bottle's done. Okay, *now* it's time to clean up.'"

As the babies grew, King took on more responsibilities. For the first few months, except at naptimes, the youngsters had the run of the house and Pat relied on King's ability to keep them occupied and out of trouble. Lion and tiger cubs are mischief-machines but they are also very affectionate, just like domestic dogs and cats. According to Pat, young lions in particular are very dog-like. "Actually, we have one lion, Zamba — he's 10 years old now — that slept in bed with us until he was about eight months old."

With King as a playmate and guardian, the energy of these growing felines had a safe outlet, and during the time they lived in the house they were often found snuggling up next to their canine nanny. Even later, in their permanent homes outdoors, they always welcomed King when he accompanied Joe and Pat as they worked about the farm.

It didn't take long before the Bergerons earned a reputation in the zoo world as people who would consider taking animals no one else wanted. And there are more such animals than most people realize. While many zoos have responsible breeding and conservation programs, others cater first and foremost to the viewing public. Lion cubs, for example, are a popular draw to zoo-goers. Unfortunately, there are more zoo-bred lions than there are zoos to house them, so when those cute cubs mature, it's a challenge to place them successfully. Animals with chronic conditions, such as blindness, lameness, or even old age, are not as "viewer-friendly" to visitors who demand young, perfect specimens. If a suitable buyer for these animals isn't found, euthanasia is often the only option. And many exotic animals need special diets or living conditions, without which they become ill. Psychological and social needs can be even more difficult to meet, especially for animals that normally live in large groups. The Bergerons began to get calls about all sorts of special-needs animals. Their farm became known as "the place for animals with nowhere to go."

"A lot of our animals are surplus from zoos," says Pat. "Others have come because of health problems." For instance, eight years ago they took two Siberian tigers, Nogi and Kong, rejected from another zoo because they were blind. The blindness, they discovered, was due to cataracts, probably resulting from dietary deficiencies. "We got donations so both of them could have cataract surgery," says Pat.

Local humane societies began calling, too. Exotic animals have always had a certain caché for people wanting something out of the ordinary. Unfortunately, few such animals make good long-term domestic companions. A baby monkey is irresistibly cute, but when it grows up to destroy the living room, eliminate on the walls, and attack people, it's not a pet — it's a disaster. Exotic cats, which possess all the skills necessary for jungle survival, can be horrifically destructive in the average home. So outdoor enclosures house the Bergeron's big cats — six tigers, six lions, four jaguars, eight cougars — as well as two more servals that aren't tame enough for the house.

One by one, animals kept coming. "We don't raise as many babies now," says Pat. "Our house is full of humane society rescues." Besides their six domestic cats they have three African servals, an Asian jungle cat, and an F1 Bengal — a first-generation cross between an Asian leopard cat and a domestic cat — most of whom also grew up in King's care. "He's really good about the small cats," she says, adding that these smaller exotic cats can be a challenge to domesticate. Because the big cats have few predators, they are very laid-back and relaxed; small cats are, by nature, more wary. "Especially the African servals," says Pat. "They require respect!" Even though her cats are several generations away from the wild, they retain the cautious independence their feral relatives rely on to survive. But inside, under King's watchful eye, they coexist in peace.

They've also taken in wolves, foxes, and lynx. In one outdoor habitat lives a coatimundi, a raccoon-like mammal indigenous to Central and South America. A young man had found the animal in a Toronto pet shop. He kept it in his apartment for about a year and a half before he realized he couldn't provide the environment this animal needed. "He looked all over until he found us," recalls Pat.

Then there are the birds. "We have a Great Horned Owl and two Eurasian Eagle Owls which are even bigger than the Great Horned Owl," says Pat. In the aviary, parrots of every kind flit from branch to branch, all relinquished by private owners.

"We also have two beautiful, big, male baboons, seven Japanese macaques (snow monkeys), a whole bunch of goats, a donkey named Amigo, two highland cows, and a black bear named Edna," Pat says, counting as she surveys the pens, trying not to miss anyone. "Oh, and we got these ground squirrels about a month ago," she adds. "We're going to build them an outdoor enclosure in the spring."

It's a lot of work. "It's only me, Joe, my daughter, and our daughter-in-law," says Pat. "We do need some staff on a full-time basis. I'm out working with the animals by nine in the morning, and don't come in until four-thirty or five when it's getting dark." Until about a decade ago, their work was funded largely by donations. Then they opened their sanctuary to paying visitors, a move that proved very successful. Each summer, admission fees from enthusiastic and appreciative guests helped ensure the winter feed bills will be paid.

Unfortunately, it didn't last. Pressure from a small group of very vocal opponents, backed by a handful of county councillors, resulted in the sanctuary being accused of zoning by-law infractions. Despite approval from the Canadian Association of Zoos and Aquariums, despite much favourable publicity generated by Toronto Sun columnist Peter Worthington, and despite the staunch support of the volunteer group Friends of Bergerons, the sanctuary was forced to close their doors until expensive upgrades were completed and rezoning had gone through. It was a harsh blow, one they've not yet recovered from.

To the Bergerons' relief, donations keep trickling in. They try not to worry about their unsettled future. The passion they have for this work keeps them going. Over the years, they have learned more about animal abuse and neglect than they ever wanted to know and they refuse to let municipal squabbles derail their purpose. "We got a call about two Japanese macaques, Chico and Anna," says Pat. When one of the owners died, the other lost enthusiasm and began leaving them with various friends and relatives, none of whom were even remotely interested in keeping them. And even in the depths of winter, the macaques had no shelter and inadequate food.

The day the animals were brought to the sanctuary, the Bergerons watched in horror as the young man punched Chico about the head. This, he told them, was how they kept the monkeys in line. But that wasn't the worst. The monkeys were both addicted to the cigarette butts given to them in a misguided attempt to deworm them. Anna had been fed percocet, a potent narcotic, possibly to keep her quiet. Her first month with the Bergerons was spent in the agony of withdrawal. "They were so thin," recalls Pat. "They hadn't had proper food, and they'd been teased so badly. They were in horrible condition both physically and psychologically." Today they are strong and healthy, but they will never be whole emotionally. All Pat and Joe can do is give them a safe place to live out their lives.

Another macaque named Lexi arrived addicted to a cough syrup containing codeine, another narcotic. "The people told me to give her some whenever she coughed," says Pat. Besides the chemical addiction, Lexi had the mysterious habit of crouching with her head craned upwards. Even in her spacious new enclosure, it took several weeks before she stopped exhibiting this behaviour. "It turns out they'd kept her in a clothes hamper," explains Pat.

With King at her side, Pat walks from one enclosure to another, listing the animals inside and where they came from. She pauses at the enclosure where Casey and Axel, now 17 and 16 but still youthful and healthy, wave their tails in greeting. "I'd never in a million years have imagined it would have turned out like this!" she says with a smile. "It just happened."

She absent-mindedly strokes the head of the big dog next to her, her silent partner. "If people are being hurt and abused they can tell someone," Pat says quietly. "Animals can't." In a wordless show of support, King gets up to follow her as she moves on. There's no question that he's there to help, any way he can.

Chapter 4
Breaking Through Autism

The shoe rack overflows in the Kimber household in Nobleton, Ontario. Running shoes pile against hockey skates; kicked-off snow boots lean against a heap of winter jackets. With five children and two adults milling about, there are a lot of feet in the house already; you might not expect them to welcome four more. But when Rose Kimber got the news that they were only weeks away from adding a service dog to their family, she couldn't sleep for excitement. She didn't know its name, whether it was male or female, or even what breed it was. All she knew was that they were nearing the end of a two-year wait and that this dog would change their lives.

Nancy Ambrogio of London, Ontario, had a very different reaction to the suggestion that she get a service dog for her son Michael. When Michael's kindergarten teacher brought up the subject, Nancy's first thought was, "I don't need one more thing to complicate my life!" She had little experience and no particular interest in dogs, but the real problem was that she already had more than enough to fill each day; how could she look after a dog, too?

Tim and Trish Brown of Ayr, near Kitchener, were already weighing the pros and cons of service dogs when their son inadvertently sealed the deal. Matthew was a seasoned escape artist already, but his parking lot escapade was the last straw. When they heard that specially-trained dogs help keep such kids out of danger, they knew they had no choice. Matthew had to get a service dog.

Each of these families has several children, and a youngest son with autism. They all travelled the same frustrating and confusing road to proper diagnosis and help. And for all three boys and their families, help came on four legs, thanks to National Service Dogs.

* * *

When Rose Kimber took Arik, her fourth child, for his 18-month checkup, the doctor wondered aloud if Arik might be a bit behind in his speech development. An experienced mother, Rose ignored the suggestion. She knew that children mature at their own rate. Perhaps Arik was just a late bloomer. The doctor wasn't overly concerned either, and the subject was dropped.

But by the time Arik was two, they'd noticed a few unusual behaviours. He held objects in his hands while simultaneously spinning them. He stood at the open cupboard, as if mesmerized by the contents. He meticulously sorted his toys into different piles. Rose, pregnant with their youngest child, made a mental note of these behaviours. Then a nasty bout of pneumonia landed Arik in hospital. At that time his language development was still delayed, but between the trauma of hospitalization and the adjustment to the new baby shortly after, these behaviours were easy to understand. He'd catch up, they convinced themselves, as soon as things settled down.

But he didn't. "That's when the word 'autism' first came up," says Rose. By Arik's second birthday, she had to face the fact that her little boy had special needs. "I started to look into what this thing called autism really is."

Then the pieces began to fall into place. Although he displayed affection, he rarely made eye contact, and he was intensely sensitive to noise, both classic traits of autism. The sound of a motor-boat or a chain saw or even the vacuum cleaner made him hysterical. He cried uncontrollably, hid under the bed, did whatever he had to do to get as far away from the noise as possible.

There were other clues as well. "He has no sense of danger," Rose says. Without constant vigilance, Arik was likely to wander off or run out into traffic. "He also has an extremely high pain tolerance," she adds. When Arik was about three, during a stay at their cottage, Rose noticed he was walking strangely. Although he hadn't complained, she sat him down and looked at his bare feet. She was horrified to find splinters covering the soles of his feet, many of them deeply embedded in his flesh. "We spent an hour at the clinic, having slivers dug out of his feet with a needle," recalls Rose. "The slivers didn't bother him — but holding him down, that made him scream."

Arik became well-known amongst their cottage neighbours that summer. Like many autistic kids, he was extremely sensitive to texture. Some children become tactile-seeking, wanting to feel a certain object over and over. Others, like Arik, become tactile-aversive, disliking or avoiding certain textures. "He hated wearing clothes, especially socks," says Rose. His favourite trick was to run over to the cottage next door and then take off all his clothes. "That was probably the hardest summer," says Rose. "Our youngest was one by then, and mobile, so I had to watch the baby plus I had this toddler who was constantly taking off."

Around that time Rose learned of an organization that trains dogs to assist people with various disabilities. Both she and her husband are experienced dog people, having been involved in a variety of dog sports, from flyball and agility, to sledding and Schutzhund. "My husband and I used to breed and train German shepherd dogs," says Rose. "We actually met working through dog training." What excited her was the fact that National Service Dogs trained dogs especially for the unique needs of autistic children and their families. She commenced the complex application process. "They wanted a video of Arik, a letter from his pediatrician, letters from each parent, and a reference letter from a friend," she says. "It was a lot of work to do when we were busy just trying to deal with life in general!" But she knew that if they were accepted onto the waiting list, it would be worth it.

The following year they received official notice of acceptance: they were now in line for a dog. It was time to begin raising money. While no one is refused a dog on financial grounds, each family that receives a dog from NSD tries to help support the intensive training costs. By the time the Kimbers were on the list, $12,000 went into each dog. "We spent the next couple of years fund-raising," she says. "My kids got very involved. They gave up birthday gifts and they asked for donations to the dog fund, in order to support their brother." They were proud to contribute to the process. Rose emphasized that the dog they eventually got would be Arik's dog, not a family pet. Although she left open the possibility that they might get another dog later on, the kids agreed that the service dog came first.

NSD places two groups of dogs each year. Rose didn't know where they were on the list, but hoped they would be in the Spring 2005 group. Then, in September of 2004 they heard the thrilling news. "We've got a dog for you."

Rose and the other excited recipients arrived at the centre on a Sunday night, eager to begin their week-long training. They were given an itinerary and sent to bed. None of them knew anything, yet, about their dogs.

On Monday morning the group gathered at the kennel. Black labs, yellow labs, and golden retrievers met them with an enthusiastic chorus of barks and yelps. "They introduced all the dogs and let each of us work with all the dogs in turn, to see how we interacted with all of them," says Rose. Privately she favoured a black lab named Gus, but she trusted that the experts would match her with the best one. The trainers had done some preliminary selections, but their final choices would be determined by observing the people with the dogs. The suspense was palpable. "Then they called us in and told us which ones were our dogs!" says Rose. "They brought me mine and I yelped, 'Really?'" It was Gus.

Right away the work began. This was no challenge for the dogs; they already knew everything. Now their new owners had to familiarize themselves with the special skills their dogs possessed. The group learned how to dress their new helpers in the special jackets identifying them as service dogs, and then they — and their eight dogs — went out for lunch. "We had to place them the right way, tuck them in, and make sure their tails wouldn't get stepped on." It was the first of many successful educational outings. By the end of the week, while many of the others were still adjusting to their new dogs, Rose felt like she'd known Gus forever.

On the last day, the group was in the food court of the nearby shopping mall. Part of their final training was to ignore food lying in front of them. They behaved perfectly! A local health news program was filming them, and while the new owners talked about their experiences, the dogs relaxed on the floor beside them. "The reporter commented that it looked like a bunch of retrievers had been shot in the food court!" Rose says.

Finally, it was time to go home and introduce Gus to Arik. Rose could hardly wait; she missed her family desperately, and she knew they were all anxious to meet this new family member. "We'd arranged it so only my son would be home when I got there," she says. "He was happy to see me. Then he said, 'Where's my dog?' I opened the back of the truck, and Arik put out his arms, giggling uncontrollably. He was laughing his face off, he was so excited. Gus went running right up to him, and Arik jumped on the dog and threw his arms around him."

They couldn't have asked for a better introduction. Most service dogs need some adjustment time before they are able to carry out all their duties, but Gus walked into the job like he'd been born to it. In his first week with the Kimber family, Rose took him with her wherever she needed to go, and he didn't turn a hair. "The first time out in public, Gus had to go into a church," says Rose. "He just crawled under a pew and went to sleep."

But it's the change in Arik that really excites Rose. "He sleeps better now that he's with Gus. In fact, the first night we had Gus, Arik slept longer than he ever has," she explains. "He slept so late, I had to take the dog when I went out. He woke up and he said he was angry because I took his dog!" From Arik, who rarely expresses his feelings, this forceful scolding was a most welcome event! "Since we've gotten Gus," adds Rose, "Arik has started making much faster progress in his speech, development, and social interaction."

Over the next week, in addition to school and church visits, Gus accompanied Rose and Arik to the speech therapist, the hockey arena, the hospital, Arik's gymnastics class, a riding stable, and a movie theatre. They also spent time at the local outdoor plaza where they introduced Gus to the community and distributed information about service dogs. Gus is the first service dog in their region, so it's a perfect public education opportunity. "People can't see anything wrong with Arik; he doesn't look disabled," says Rose. "They can't understand why I'm taking the disabled parking spot, or when they see Arik out in public they think he's misbehaving. Having a service dog with a jacket shows people there is a disability."

Because Gus would be accompanying her son to school, Rose made a special visit to introduce him to Arik's classmates. She explained that service dogs aren't like pets; they are working dogs. "When the dog's wearing his purple jacket, no one but the child or parent-handler can touch it. But when the jacket's off, that means the dog is on a break, and then they can pat him." At home, Rose relaxes the rules just enough so that during breaks, Gus can enjoy a bit of attention from the rest of the family. But at school, she's firm. Dogs need consistency and she won't allow anything to jeopardize his work with her son.

Gus definitely understands the importance of his uniform, becoming very serious and focused as soon as it slips over his head. But when the coat comes off, he's just another fun-loving retriever. "You'd almost think that he hasn't had much training because he doesn't listen very well!" she says wryly. "He's still a very young dog."

But he's a young dog making a huge difference in the life of one boy and his family. At gymnastics class, Arik participates happily with the help of a support person. Although he has the physical ability to do somersaults and walk on the balance beam, waiting in line is too much for him. "He loves to run and jump into the pit filled with giant sponges," says Rose. "He's quick to realize when he can take advantage of a distraction or an inexperienced teacher, and take off." Arik may love the thrill of the chase, but in a room full of running, jumping athletes and equipment, it's dangerous. Although they hadn't had Gus long and this was a challenging situation, Rose decided to let Arik attend the class with Gus, just to see what would happen. "Arik was amazing!" she reports. "He didn't take off! He'd pat Gus, or lay on top of Gus until it was his turn, then he'd do 10 different things in sequence, and come back." The coaches could hardly believe this was the same hair-raising child. With Gus, Arik had something to focus on while awaiting his turn.

When Rose watches her son sleeping soundly with his dog, or giggling at the soft, wet tongue on his hands, or lolling on the floor with him, she knows they got lucky. Gus is a particularly bright dog and he very quickly developed a strong bond with both Arik and the entire family and it helps that they all liked dogs to begin with. But still, they asked a great deal of their new friend, and he didn't hesitate to respond. "For me, Gus is an extra set of hands," says Rose. "He's accomplished more for me in two weeks than some dogs do in a year. I just know he'll be there." Four more feet, it seems, have more than earned their keep.

* * *

When Michael Ambrogio was born in 1995, his siblings were 15, 13, and 2; like many last-born children, he was often referred to simply as "the baby." His mother Nancy knew from experience how quickly the early months and years fly by. She'd enjoyed a healthy pregnancy, had an easy delivery, and expected to savour parenting this last child of hers. But as Michael grew, she noticed differences between him and the other children.

"He made very fast motor milestones compared to my other kids," recalls Nancy. Her first three children walked late, but talked early. Michael was walking, but his vocabulary wasn't developing. By his first birthday, she expected him to recognize things like balloons and candles. Her other children had all been able to hold up a finger to show how old they were. "Michael didn't do any of that," says Nancy. "He just wasn't interested." She kept taking him for check-ups and the doctors kept telling her to relax, implying she was overprotective and that if she'd quit helping him, he'd learn to talk like everyone else. But when he still wasn't conversing by his second birthday, Nancy listened to her instincts and took him in for a full-blown assessment. The news was devastating. "We learned that he had the receptive communication skills of a seven-month old," she says. "Expressively, he was at an even lower level because he was almost completely non-verbal." Even now, eight years later, it's hard for her to talk about that day.

They knew now that something was wrong with Michael, but even after a visit to a pediatric development specialist, they still had no diagnosis. Speech therapy, at a cost of 60 dollars an hour, brought no improvement. Finally they got a referral to a specialist at Toronto's Hospital for Sick Children. In November of 1999, they got their answer. "Michael was diagnosed with classic autism, under the Autism Spectrum Disorder," says Nancy. "This is exactly what I was hoping *not* to hear, but it was helpful at least to get a diagnosis. It gave us something concrete, instead of hoping to one day wake up and have him be normal."

With a special therapy called Intensive Behavioural Intervention, or IBI, Michael's development finally began to progress. But soon after he began with IBI, they were told that Michael was no longer eligible for the therapy under the Ontario health care system. "His uphill gains plateaued at that time," remembers Nancy. "Now specific skills are hit-and-miss, and it's hard for him to maintain what he's learned."

Then a chocolate Labrador retriever named Shelby came into his life. It took a little persuading for Nancy to even consider the idea of having a dog. But then she and Michael attended a workshop on service dogs. "Michael had the opportunity to touch the dog, and he went gaga over him, cuddled right up on the ground with him," says Nancy. "We knew then that we had to have one." Even with no other advantages, she knew any extra work would be worthwhile simply to see him so happy. But from what she'd heard, there were many practical ways a dog could help her son — and the entire family.

Like many autistic children, Michael has no sense of danger. The only place they are sure he's safe is at home, where the environment is controlled. "We have alarms on all our doors," says Nancy. "He was a shut-in. He went to school, and he came home for his therapy. I couldn't take him anywhere because I couldn't be sure what his response would be. What if he had a melt-down somewhere? What if he took off and I couldn't get to him?"

In November 2001, Shelby came to live with them. Immediately they noticed changes in Michael's behaviour, especially around other people. "He has much more spontaneous language now," reports Nancy. "If someone points to me and asks who I am, he won't say 'Mom,' but if someone asks him what his dog's name is, he'll answer 'Shelby' one hundred percent of the time."

But it's the simple things — going to the grocery store, crossing the street — that have changed most. Securely tethered to his dog, Michael can't run out into traffic or dart away from his parents, nor is he likely to try. Somehow, when he's with Shelby he's calmer. And the fact that he's attached to a dog clearly identified as a service animal makes it easier for strangers to understand Michael's actions. "Although he looks normal, his behaviour isn't normal, and this makes it hard for people who don't know him," explains Nancy. "I had to do something to identify Michael as a child that's different and needs protection."

The other big benefit to Michael is that Shelby's winning ways attract positive attention. He's forced to talk to people, and his dog is an easy topic. Even his schoolmates are more comfortable talking with him, now that Shelby is there.

Six months after getting Shelby, Nancy and Michael stood in line at the airport. Crowds milled about them. Strange noises filled the air. As Nancy walked past the conveyor belt loaded with luggage, she marvelled at the change in both her and her son. Holding tightly to his dog, Michael was anxious but controlled. He didn't attempt to leave Nancy's side, but if he had, Nancy knew Shelby would act as an anchor. "Michael and I and Shelby flew to Sault Ste. Marie, something I wouldn't even have let cross my mind before

Shelby!" she says. "So, that's another big benefit: Michael has had more experiences as a result of having Shelby."

* * *

Tim and Trish Brown were looking forward to parenthood, but when contractions began more than a month early, their excitement turned to fear. It was too soon. They rushed to Kitchener's Grand River Hospital where doctors discovered Trish was on the verge of a stroke. With the lives of both mother and baby at stake, doctors decided to induce labour.

On November 22, 1994, their son entered the world, fragile but determined. "Matthew was born six weeks premature, weighing in at 5 pounds, 13 ounces," remembers Trish. "He'd experienced some breathing difficulties and complications associated with respiratory distress syndrome, so he was emergency airlifted to the neonatal unit at Hamilton's McMaster Hospital four hours after his birth." There, neonatal specialists and medical technology helped him through the crisis. Tubes, tape, wires, and equipment nearly covered his tiny body, and he was kept under constant sedation.

"When I arrived at McMaster's Neonatal Unit," says Tim, "having prayed my heart out during my drive from Kitchener, I was met by a priest, a doctor, and a social worker. I refused to believe the worst had happened. That's when I was taken aside and told the seriousness of the situation."

Trish couldn't bear to be separated from her baby.

Hours after her difficult labour and delivery, she signed herself out of the Kitchener hospital and joined her husband in the Hamilton neonatal unit. Trish had not heard Matthew's voice. She hadn't held him. She didn't even know what colour his eyes were. "The baby was given a fifty percent chance of survival," says Trish.

But Matthew was a fighter. His breathing difficulties responded to treatment and he didn't develop any of the other problems associated with premature birth. Soon he was even gaining weight. "Eighteen days later, on December 12th, we brought him home," says Trish, "just in time for Christmas."

The Browns settled in to the ordinary tasks of parenting a new baby, overwhelmed with relief at having their son back, healthy and happy. But their peace would be short-lived. "One day, when he was about two months old, Matthew stopped breathing," says Trish. "I called 911, and he was rushed to the hospital." Doctors concluded that only his mother's quick action had prevented Matthew from becoming a victim of Sudden Infant Death Syndrome. The family heaved a sigh of relief. Surely now the worst was over.

Then a new concern crept up. "The first few months of his development seemed normal, but at nine months Matthew began having difficulty eating — gagging, vomiting, and on more than one occasion, even choking on baby foods." Trish and Tim were bewildered at this strange problem. They hadn't gone through this with their other four boys and had no idea why a child would have such extraordinary difficulty with such an ordinary event. It wouldn't be until much later, and many other clues, that they would be given an explanation.

Other developmental delays gradually became apparent. Matthew's walking, talking, and even age-appropriate play all lagged behind that of other children his age. But Matthew's emotional development alarmed them most. "He never wanted affection," says Trish, "nor would he return it." It also bothered them that even when they could see he'd hurt himself, he showed no signs of pain.

In spite of his many challenges, Matthew wasn't *sick*; he just wasn't quite well. Perhaps all these symptoms were related to his traumatic birth. "Don't worry so much," they were told. "He'll probably grow out of it."

During his toddler years, Matthew's developmental delays became more apparent. He had little social interaction with children his own age. He was hyperactive. Finally, after extensive investigation of his eating and sleeping disorders at Toronto's Hospital for Sick Children, the Browns had an initial diagnosis. "The doctor called Matthew's condition Sensory Regulatory Disorder," says Trish. "But, unfortunately, SRD requires early intervention. Matthew was almost three by then."

Further testing brought even worse results: Matthew was diagnosed with borderline mental retardation. Each expert seemed to explain part of Matthew's behaviour but none of them put the pieces together in a way that reflected a true picture of their son. Something was being missed.

For the next couple of years they kept searching for answers. Finally Matthew was referred to Children's Hospital in London and, after a year on a waiting list, the doctor who assessed him called them into his office. With trepidation, Tim and Trish sat down and prepared themselves for his news. They knew it wasn't likely to be good. "At the age of six," says Trish, "and after numerous assessments, Matt was diagnosed with Autism Spectrum Disorder, attention deficit hyperactivity disorder, and phonological and separation anxiety disorder." All the pieces of the puzzle fell into place. Even his early eating problems made sense. Sensory issues relating to texture commonly cause eating problems with autistic children. "We had an answer to the problems Matthew was experiencing, but this in no way diminished the challenges we faced back then, and still face to this day."

The biggest challenge was, and is, Matthew's tendency to bolt. "He's considered a flight risk, which means he will run off without notice," says Trish, "and he has. Too many times to recall, he's broken away from us and dashed out into traffic." After many near misses, they decided family outings were simply not worth the stress. It was a rare treat for both of them to attend an event together; their other children understood that only one parent would ever be cheering at the sidelines. The other would be at home with Matthew.

But that was before Cooper. "I first learned of National

66

Matthew Brown with Cooper

Service Dogs through a member of our local Autism Society of Ontario chapter," says Trish. This member also understood all too well the safety issues Trish and Tim faced, and encouraged them to consider applying for a dog. "This would be a solution to the bolting problem which would afford us the opportunity to get out more often with less concern for his safety," says Trish. And although Matthew's improved safety would be the main benefit, they'd also heard that some kids slept better with a dog, and they hoped this would be the case with Matthew.

They discussed the idea with Matthew, explaining that this dog would be a friend and a helper, not a pet. He and the dog would be a team, but he would have to cooperate in order for the dog to do its job. He liked animals, and he'd already had a cat. Matthew's reaction was even better than Trish and Tim had hoped: he was thrilled!

The day before Matthew turned 10, Cooper arrived with big sloppy kisses for the birthday boy. As Tim and Trish tucked their son and his new friend into bed for the night, they crossed their fingers. "The first night with Cooper, Matthew slept through the entire night for the first time in nine years," says Trish. "To this day, it continues to be the norm."

The family now goes out in public together, with Matthew tethered securely to Cooper. Not only is he unable to bolt, it no longer has the appeal it once did. Who would want to run away when such a wonderful dog is standing next to you?

* * *

Cooper, Shelby, and Gus have achieved something for their special boys that no one else has been able to do. They are truly miracle workers.

Chapter 5
The Wisdom
of Donkeys

e'd been lying in a field for 10 days, barely able to lift his head. His hooves were so over-grown he could no longer walk. In despera-tion, he'd begun hobbling to food and water on his knees, but by the time Sandra Pady of the Donkey Sanctuary of Canada was called, Trooper, as they named him, had nearly given up. He'd spent so much time on the ground that huge infected sores had developed on his body. He was malnourished and in tremendous pain from the joint and tendon damage resulting from trying to walk on such deformed hooves.

"In all our 11 years of operation," says Sandra, "we'd never admitted a donkey in such desperate condition." Trooper had to be lifted into the trailer and carried to his new home at the sanctuary near Guelph.

It took over two weeks of constant care before they even knew if Trooper would live. The excess hoof growth was immediately removed, but not all the damage was so easily reversed. "Trooper was able to stand only for brief periods and even that was possible only with assistance from our staff and volunteers," says Sandra. "His sores were treated daily and he was given pain medication." After careful trimming by a farrier, corrective shoes were made for Trooper's front hooves to help him regain his mobility.

A year later he's a new animal. He stands and moves without pain. His sores have all healed and he's regained the sparkle in his eye. "Trooper is doing marvellously well," says Sandra. "He's 100 percent recovered." As his health improved, Trooper's affectionate nature showed through, making him a favourite with visitors. It's been a long haul but he made it and now it's his turn to give something back.

At the sanctuary, these needy donkeys and mules are given one last chance for health and happiness and, in return, they bring joy to visitors, help people with handicaps develop skills, and assist in educating students about animal welfare.

Each week during the spring and summer, a group of students with special needs makes their way into the fields. They couldn't ask for a more beautiful, tranquil classroom; lessons take place under serene skies, surrounded by 100 acres of rolling hillside, carved with meandering paths, and dotted with shade-trees and flower-filled meadows. Here and there, small herds of donkeys graze contentedly. "In the Life

Skills program," explains Sandra, "young people perform various tasks according to their abilities. Some help with minor barn chores, others groom donkeys, and for some, it's just an opportunity to interact with the animals." Working with the donkeys increases the students' confidence, and teachers report improvement in many areas, even memory, when they come regularly over the course of several weeks.

"Our Animal Welfare Education Program is an Ontario curriculum-based program for junior-kindergarten to grade three," says Sandra. The sanctuary prepares the kids beforehand with written information and activity ideas, and then the youngsters come to visit the donkeys for some hands-on learning. "We're anxious to make any kind of connection with young people and to help them see animals in a situation where they are more than just sources of meat or milk," Sandra adds. "Humans should have relationships of caring, positive stewardship with other animals. We're on a mission here!"

Years ago, this mission was nothing more than a dream. As a child, Sandra Pady couldn't bear to see animals in distress. Every beast languishing in a field, or left out in the cold or sweltering heat, lingered in her mind for days. If she suspected an animal was being neglected, the frustration and helplessness nearly drove her mad. She vowed that when she grew up she would make a difference.

When Sandra and her husband purchased a large farm, she knew her dream of rescuing animals in distress could become a reality. But Sandra's first opportunity came unexpectedly.

A neighbouring farmer had purchased a donkey in the hope that it would protect his goat-herd from predators. A single donkey, usually a female or "jennet" (often called a jenny), can be a very effective guard for cattle, sheep, or goats if she becomes attached to the herd. Once she's bonded with the animals she'll protect them as she would her own offspring. This donkey, however, was a male with no attachment to the goats, and he felt no compulsion to protect them. When the disappointed farmer lost interest, the donkey was removed from the herd and left alone in a stall, a terrible punishment for a long-lived, sociable animal.

When Sandra learned about the donkey, she arranged to purchase him and thus, Sebastian became the first resident at what would soon become the Donkey Sanctuary of Canada. Through caring for this lonely donkey, Sandra quickly learned to love this fascinating cousin of the horse. Donkeys, or asses as they were once known, make gentle, loving pets and can be excellent stable companions for horses and other animals. Mules are donkey hybrids, the offspring of a male donkey and a female horse. In the case of a male horse bred to a female donkey, the offspring is called a hinny. Mules and hinnies are usually sterile.

Sandra had barely begun her training in donkey lore when she learned about a small herd of donkeys about to be sold to a slaughterhouse. She immediately set about rescuing them as well. Suddenly, 16 donkeys were grazing in her field.

She was discovering what others already know:

"longears," as aficionados call them, are addictive. Miniature donkey breeder Karen Pollard, of Keepsake Farm in Acton, is effusive in her praise of these little equines. "I think donkeys are the unsung heroes of the animal world," she says. "Most of the world's transportation is still by donkey." She credits their reputation as guardians to the fact that they don't run to protect themselves. "They confront danger, or actively seek it out," she says. "They are the natural enemy of anything canine."

Very little escapes their attention, and they have an amazing ability to communicate within a herd. "Just check out the ears on them," Karen says. "They're like radar! Each ear flick is a direct message." One afternoon, she happened to glance out her window in time to witness an example of the communication and teamwork used by her herd of 30-some donkeys. Karen uses electric fencing around her fields and the donkeys know to stay away from it, allowing the grass along the fence-line to grow very tall. As her farm is surrounded by many other homes, new neighbours frequently arrive, many of whom bring dogs with them. Each of these finds the temptation of an open field next door irresistible — until the donkeys come on the scene.

That day, an unfamiliar dog was exploring the far side of the field, unacquainted with the resident herd. Karen knew the donkeys couldn't reach the dog in time to hurt him, so she watched to see how the encounter would pan out. Very casually and quietly, the donkeys aligned themselves in single file, foals and all, and began a stealth-march under cover of the tall grass along the electric fence. The dog, preoccupied with some enticing barnyard smell, didn't notice a thing. "Alexander the Great would have been proud!" Karen says, with a laugh. "Suddenly, as if led by some unspoken command of *'Charge!'* the donkeys rushed out of the tall grass with ears back to confront the intruder, as if breathing fire out their nostrils. After the dog landed from his initial 10-foot launch perpendicular into the air, he broke both the sound barrier and the record for a long distance leap by a canine."

Then the donkeys nodded to each other as if in congratulations on the well-organized and well-executed rout, turned, and walked nonchalantly back up the field. "It was just another day on the endless job of keeping all strange canines at bay!" says Karen. The dog, she adds, never returned. He'd learned his lesson and had no intention of asking for a re-match with the ghost-like long-eared dragons on the other side of the fence. Karen deliberately encourages this protective behaviour in her animals, and many of them are successfully put to work as guardians. But, as with Sebastian, it doesn't always work. Not everyone is willing to hang on to an animal that isn't earning his keep.

Sandra Pady hadn't particularly intended for her farm to become a donkey sanctuary, but as her herd grew, the idea grew with it. When friends mentioned the donkey sanctuaries in England, she did some serious research and got in touch with Dr. Elizabeth Svendsen, founder of the non-profit

Donkey Sanctuary, in Great Britain. The largest such refuge in the world, Dr. Svendsen's sanctuary has given countless equines a lifelong home; thousands of human visitors have learned about their gentle, winning ways. Dr. Svendsen encouraged Sandra and gave her advice on how to create a proper sanctuary of her own.

Sandra's Donkey Sanctuary of Canada embraces the philosophy that donkeys have intrinsic value and deserve the opportunity to live out their lives free from want or need, surrounded by their own kind, in a protected, natural environment.

Donkeys come in three sizes, as Sandra soon learned. Horse-sized donkeys, over 140 centimetres at the withers, or shoulder, are referred to as mammoth donkeys. The diminutive miniature donkeys measure less than 90 cm, whereas standards are between 90 and 140 cm. "Paco is the tiniest donkey ever brought to the DSC," says Sandra. Born with a deformed jaw, Paco was unable to nurse and had to be bottle-fed. He became imprinted on his owner to the point where he had no interest in other donkeys. "After about six months, his guardian contacted us, and Paco was brought to the sanctuary," says Sandra. Paco, unfortunately, didn't want to be with donkeys; he wanted to be with people! Somehow, they had to teach him to fit in with the herd. Sandra introduced him to a jenny with a new foal. Paco reluctantly acquiesced, but it wasn't until Chiclet arrived that his true education began.

"Paco was about two or three years old when Chiclet

came to farm as a six-month old foal," says Sandra. Like Paco, he'd also spent too much time alone; he'd apparently been abandoned in a field to survive the winter as best he could. By the time he made it to the sanctuary in early spring, his hooves were overgrown, he was covered with ticks, and frostbite had destroyed the ends of both ears. After some intensive care, he was soon running around the barnyard, curious about the other donkeys. One in particular caught his eye. "From the moment of arrival," says Sandra, "Chiclet decided Paco was his pal." Paco wasn't impressed with this hanger-on but Chiclet, encouraged by the staff, persisted in his overtures of friendship. Because Paco ate so slowly and couldn't compete with the bigger animals, they felt he might benefit from having a big "brother" by his side. "Paco isn't a strong donkey by any stretch," says Sandra. "When he's in with the main herd he can get lost in the jumble." As Chiclet grew, Paco found he had no choice but to accept his new friend. Eventually, Paco even learned to play with him. Paco still likes to think he's human, but Chiclet doesn't let him get away with it for long. Perhaps Chiclet knows that little Paco, for all his bravado, needs someone looking out for him.

The farm's many visitors bond closely with the donkeys, some eventually volunteering time or financial support to help care for their special friends. "Pansy and Poppy are our best ambassadors," says Sandra of one mother-daughter donkey pair. "These two tolerate no end of hugging and kissing." Pansy is a miniature donkey who spent the first four years of her life alone and neglected on a farm outside Montreal. She was rescued and brought into her first new home, where she gave birth to Poppy. The two donkeys lived there contentedly until the owner was forced to sell her farm and the donkeys moved to the sanctuary.

Pansy and Poppy are very protective of each other, showing little interest in the other donkeys. Yet, whenever visitors come to the farm, they immediately trot over with a loving nuzzle and an offer to be brushed.

Their immaculate behaviour has even earned them invitations to church! "In the Christian tradition," says Sandra, "Mary rode into Bethlehem on a donkey and Jesus rode into Jerusalem on one. It's not unusual for churches to contact us for Palm Sunday services." The donkeys inject a touch of realism to the pageantry as they delicately pick their way up the greenery-strewn centre aisle of a church, surrounded by costumed children.

Poppy and Pansy have an intuitive ability to gauge a situation and react accordingly. "One spring about five years ago," remembers Sandra, "we got a call about a woman who was in the final stages of cancer." The woman had been a long-time supporter, both with her time and her money, and her illness had progressed rapidly. A friend told Sandra that the woman missed the donkeys, but couldn't easily get to the farm from her Toronto home anymore. "She wondered if there was a way she could see them one last time," says Sandra. They put their heads together and came up with a plan. If she couldn't come to the donkeys, the donkeys would go to her.

Sandra brushed Poppy and Pansy until they shone, wove fresh peony blossoms into their halters and loaded them onto a trailer. "We ended up taking them into downtown Toronto, where they walked so sweetly, we were able to lead them right into the woman's backyard. She spent a perfectly joyous hour with them." A month later she died. For one short hour, two little donkeys replaced her fear and loneliness with joy. Few who've met Poppy and Pansy doubt that they understood the importance of their task.

Karen Pollard has great respect for the innate wisdom of these little animals. Her miniature donkey, Sparkle, purchased from a retiring farmer, showed her just how astute they can be. "Sparkle, though well-loved and looked after, was basically feral in behaviour with anyone that stepped into her paddock," says Karen. The little donkey did not appreciate being rounded up and snatched away from the only home she'd ever known. "She was unforgiving," says Karen. "No amount of sweet-talking and treat-feeding from me would get the look off her face that said, 'You yanked me away from all that was safe once, and you could do it again!'" She eventually settled in to her new home and even became comfortable with visitors to the farm — especially if they offered treats — but nothing would convince her to trust Karen.

Sparkle had several foals over the years, offspring to whom she faithfully passed on her lifetime grudge. Other people were welcome to pet and fuss over the babies, but not Karen. "Whenever she saw me, she quickly herded them away." These had always been male foals, destined to be gelded and sold. But one year Sparkle gave birth to a female foal Karen wanted to keep. She knew she couldn't have another donkey that hated her. So with the help of a friend Sparkle trusted, she formulated a plan and took drastic action. When the baby was only a few hours old, Karen's friend coaxed Sparkle and her newborn into a small pen, where Karen planned to work her charm. "Donkeys being intuitively wise, as soon as Sparkle saw me, she knew what was up," says Karen.

She expected Sparkle to stay between her and the baby, beginning the indoctrination into the "Karen as evil incarnate" school of thought. "Imagine my shock when Sparkle dropped her nose and gingerly nudged her wet, wobbly little prize towards me!" she says. She held her breath, trying not to break the magic playing out before her eyes. But Sparkle calmly allowed her foal to sniff and nuzzle Karen and accept the strokes she offered. "After the baby had ingested a good healthy smell of me, I reached out to see if Sparkle had finally forgiven me. She recoiled as if to say, 'You and I will always have issues, but I know you will look after my baby, as you have me. I can't get over the past but, for the good of everyone, my baby can.'"

It was a moment Karen will never forget. "Wars handed down from generation to generation would no longer exist," she says thoughtfully. "Feuds and hard feelings would just die out with the passing of each generation. Humans could learn a lot about peace-making from animals."

Chapter 6
Teegan the Superdog

hush falls over the crowd. Into the ring bursts Teegan, an elegant standard poodle, his apricot-coloured coat trimmed and shaped to perfection. He prances from foot to foot while he waits for his owner, Morgan Jarvis of Bowmanville, to give the word. The whistle blows. "Let's go, Teegan!"

It's the Superdog Show, and it's jam-packed with excitement for spectators and handlers, but especially for the dogs. Responding to Morgan's hand signals and voice commands, Teegan leaps over jumps and across hurdles, blasts through tunnels, and scrambles over the six-foot tall A-frame obstacle. He rounds a corner at full speed, and faces a jump most dogs — and probably a few horses — would balk at. It's made up of two end pieces with poles stacked across them.

In competition, small dogs jump the lowest height, perhaps one or two poles. Large dogs jump proportionately higher hurdles. Teegan has already mastered the highest jumps in the standard agility trials; now he's going for the record — 10 poles balanced on brightly painted sidepieces. The slightest jostle will knock them off.

Teegan straightens out to approach the jump at full speed. He gathers his hind-quarters to prepare for the spring, stretches out to an impossible length, curves his front paws over the topmost pole, arches his back, tucks his hind legs in, and glides over the topmost pole with a hair's-breadth to spare. He lands smoothly, springing up and on to the final obstacle. Applause explodes from the spectators. Teegan jumps up to kiss the woman he loves; the pair is wild with success and drunk with the crowd's approval. Then the announcement comes from the master of ceremonies: Teegan has just jumped an astounding 140 cm, over 10 bars, free and clear. It's his best jump to date and the audience goes wild. Teegan laps it up.

It takes training and conditioning to build up such an accomplished canine athlete. Many such dogs are carefully bred for generations, well-nourished from the moment of conception, and prepared from birth. Even so, only a few of these carefully nurtured contenders will achieve greatness. For dogs without the benefit of such early care, it's almost impossible to become a Superdog. Right?

Wrong! Teegan is a star today, but when Morgan first

met him he was already past puppyhood, nearing his first birthday. But he wasn't just a goofy, gangling adolescent in need of training; he was almost crippled from malnutrition and confinement. His back was so stiff that he stood hunched over, and he staggered and tripped when he tried to walk. Ignorance and neglect had left the pup emotionally starved, too. Teegan's original owner had been sent to prison shortly after he bought the puppy. He convinced his parents to take care of the pup in his absence but, unfortunately, they didn't know even the basics of dog care. They didn't realize, for instance, that standard poodles are larger than miniature poodles, so the untrained pup spent most of his time in a too-small crate, which he regularly soiled. "He was very hand-shy, as if he'd been hit in the past," Morgan adds. "And he was extremely fearful of any new situation." After a few months, the parents realized they were in over their heads and decided to board him out at the local Toronto-area kennel where Morgan worked as a groomer.

Morgan, who also ran a grooming business out of her home, will never forget the sight that greeted her that first day. "I don't think Teegan had been groomed since he was purchased at the pet store," she says. His coat was filthy and matted from head to tail. His nails were so long they'd begun to curl under his feet. Dried mucous caked his eyes. His ears were smelly, painfully infected, clogged with hair, and coated in wax and debris.

He needed a makeover, and Morgan saw to it that he got

one. First, he was thoroughly scrubbed from one end to the other. His entire coat was shaved off, a task that took several people the better part of a day. His eyes were swabbed. His nails were trimmed back to a natural length. His ears were shaved and the hair deep inside the canal was painstakingly removed. They cleaned out all the accumulated wax and dirt, topping off their meticulous grooming with medicated eardrops. Poor Teegan, whose name means "beautiful" in Welsh, was trembling with exhaustion, but he looked — and smelled — like a new dog.

Morgan changed Teegan's diet and placed him in a large run, where he could finally stretch his legs and work off some energy. With proper nutrition and exercise his health improved, and as it did, his personality began showing through. Poodles are highly intelligent and sensitive, but while they respond quickly to praise, their spirits can crumble under harsh treatment or neglect. Morgan, who already had another standard poodle and loved the breed, was drawn to him. She started taking him outside on her lunch breaks to play ball, and that's when she discovered his love for games. "I saw something special in him," says Morgan. "He was so bouncy and he played with such enthusiasm." Almost immediately the two developed a bond. "Teegan's caregivers paid for three months' care at the kennel," says Morgan. "After the three months, they decided to sign him over to me." He was a young dog, she rationalized; perhaps with proper care, he could overcome his rough start.

Some people shook their heads at Morgan. Sure, she knew dogs; she had several at home already. She was an experienced groomer and an excellent trainer. But Teegan had so many strikes against him. His early neglect and total lack of socialization could prove an insurmountable barrier to his becoming a loving and responsive companion. They were sure it would be an exercise in frustration and, ultimately, heartbreak.

Morgan ignored the nay-sayers, but the night she brought him home she began to comprehend the extent of the challenge she'd taken on. When she introduced Teegan to her other dogs, he growled at them and tried to hide behind her legs. She knew he was feeling threatened, so when she went upstairs to make a phone call, she took him with her. She sat on the bed, deep in conversation, describing to a friend how excited she was to have this new dog in her life. Teegan jumped up on the bed next to Morgan, who wasn't paying much attention to him. "All of a sudden," she says, "I felt something hot on my back!" She shrieked and leaped off the bed. Teegan had lifted his leg and urinated on her. She realized then the depths of his insecurity. Anxious at having to share the only person who loved him, Teegan staked his claim on her the only way he knew how. "This was the first and only time he displayed this behaviour," Morgan adds with relief.

It was an inauspicious beginning. He was still underweight, his eyes were droopy, and his coat was in horrible condition. But the new food was beginning to have its effect, and he gained muscle tone thanks to daily runs in the park. His physical health was improving; would his behaviour follow suit?

In the early stages of setting up her own kennel, Morgan took Teegan with her everywhere, giving him careful exposure to all sorts of new experiences. Since 1990 she'd been part of the Superdog team, one of North America's premier live entertainment events, as popular as the Harlem Globetrotters or the Ice Capades, but with dogs. The show's producers helped her facility get off the ground, and today Superdog Central, Inc. is an award winning training, grooming, and boarding kennel on seven acres in Bowmanville.

"Teegan started going to Superdog shows with me and my other dogs within a month of the time he started living with me," Morgan says. "He was under-socialized, afraid of noises, and wary of other dogs." These shows, the first of which was held at the Pacific National Exhibition in Vancouver in 1978, are intense, highly choreographed, theatrical productions in which immaculately-trained dogs execute precision movement routines set to catchy music. They run obstacle courses, leap over jumps, and thread through tunnels. Audiences rave, handlers get to show off their brilliant pooches, and the performing dogs simply love it. Teegan, however, was not impressed.

Each new noise terrified him. At every new place they visited, Teegan cowered and quaked at the end of the leash.

He startled and shied away when people reached for him. "It took over a year to get Teegan in shape," Morgan says. At first, it was enough just to acquaint Teegan with the big, wide world around him. Morgan used clicker-training, the same method of operant conditioning used by trainers of marine mammals. She taught Teegan that each "click" of the device meant he would get a treat. This allowed her to be very precise in rewarding his behaviour. Each time he entered a new building, she clicked and gave him a treat. Every time he allowed a new person to pat him, a click and another treat. "I also conditioned him with food or a toy reward when he handled threatening situations well, such as loud noises, crowds, or other animals," she adds.

With Morgan's consistent reassurance, Teegan learned to accept his canine room-mates, too. But it wasn't until the arrival of Blitz, a border collie/Jack Russell terrier cross belonging to Morgan's daughter, that he found a bosom-buddy. "They absolutely adore each other and play for hours on end," says Morgan. "Blitz is the only dog Teegan will play with." His first choice, of course, is always a game of catch with Morgan.

A year later, Teegan was living proof that the past can be overcome. From the wreckage of neglect, he emerged confident, capable, and gorgeous. Gorgeous enough, in fact, that he's become a model. He's appeared on the front page of *The Washington Post*, has been in a cellular telephone commercial, and has posed for the photos in chapter two of the popular book *Teach Yourself Visually*, by Maran Graphics & Wiley Publishing, which discusses positive reinforcement dog training.

But it's his intelligence and athleticism that have brought him true fame. Teegan's photo and an article showcasing his abilities appeared in the Iam's magazine *Your Dog*, in December 2002. The Superdog show was a highlight of the prestigious American Kennel Club/Eukanuba American Dog Classic. "His ability to run fast and jump high set his career in the Superdog Show," says Morgan. "I guess you could say he was discovered because of the show."

Teegan is currently racing in the North American Flyball Association with the multi-breed flyball team Time Bandits, who are currently in second place for the 2005 season. Flyball is a relay race in which dog teams race at breakneck speed over a row of hurdles, catch a ball, and race back to the start. It's noisy, exciting, and lots of fun. "Teegan's racing time is 4.6 seconds," boasts Morgan, "making him the fastest standard poodle in North America." His love for a good game of Frisbee® has paid off, too. He recently received his Disc Dog title with the Canadian Disc Dog Association. This dog loves his work — and it shows!

Teegan's success shows no sign of relenting. His most recent claim to fame is a small role in a full-length movie. "Teegan plays a SuperDog team member in *Daniel and the SuperDogs*, a feature length film to be released in February of 2005," says Morgan. This movie tells the heart-warming story of 11-year-old Daniel, who struggles with abandonment issues and finds solace in training his dog for an upcoming SuperDog show. Teegan is seen first in the courtroom, and later on running the obstacle course. For a dog who overcame his own abandonment issues with the help of that competition, it's a perfect fit.

Teegan may not know he's famous, but his story serves as hope to everyone everywhere who wonders if they can overcome a difficult start. His bright eyes and wagging tail tell the story: "Yes! Go for it!"

Chapter 7
Inside Their Silent World

As she walks into the kitchen, nearly 500 pounds of canine energy follow her. In the midst of four lumbering Great Danes, one all-white Jack Russell terrier leaps about impatiently, determined not to be overlooked. Lin Gardinor scolds them, motioning with her hands for them to settle down and mind their manners while she prepares their meal. Heads down, eyes rolling, they submit to Lin, properly chastened into waiting. A moment later she gives the signal and they dive into their dishes. The only sounds for several minutes are lip-smacking, crunching, and the occasional snarl from the terrier, reminding the big dogs with a curl of her lip that her food is *her* food.

Five dogs of any breed is a handful. Four Great Danes is something else; add a Jack Russell "terrorist" into the mix and the sheer volume of dog-ness rockets into the stratosphere. But the truly remarkable thing about Lin Gardinor's pack is that all of them were born hearing impaired.

Lin has long been accustomed to working with differently-abled people. For many years, she worked with a hospital-based program as a driving evaluator for people recovering from injury or illness, assessing whether or not they could get back on the road. Her job naturally led her to meet all sorts of people with special needs, some who'd had strokes or other brain injuries, others who'd been in accidents, and many who had hearing impairments. Lin, whose two children are now adults, also cared for a number of foster children over the years, some with serious disabilities. "My other children have grown up knowing I am a rescuer, so they've always had to share me with an assortment of children and animals," explains Lin.

In order to better help her clients, Lin had learned American Sign Language (ASL). She enjoyed this practical communication method and decided to try teaching it to her dog, an elderly collie-cross named Brytni. Brytni picked it up quickly, responding to a wide variety of signs. People were fascinated to watch Lin "talk" with her dog and soon the pair was invited to do demonstrations at local fairs. "Someone at the pound saw me," says Lin, "and the next time they got a deaf dog they called me." It was a frigid February when she learned they had a mostly-white Australian shepherd puppy, completely deaf, that no one wanted.

In many animals, the genetic code for white pigmentation can be a trouble-maker; in fact, it's known as the "lethal white gene." If it's kept in check by the more dominant colour genes, it can lead to some spectacular variations, such as the black-and-white harlequin seen in Great Danes, or the blue merle of Shetland sheepdogs and collies. But when two animals carrying the recessive white-gene are bred, they often produce mostly white-coated offspring that are deaf, blind, or both.

Lin already knew how her husband Ivan would react to the idea of a puppy. Brytni had numerous behavioural issues from her abusive past and Crumpet, their aging spaniel-poodle cross, had epilepsy. Surely that was enough for them to deal with.

"On this particular day I was supposed to be working in Toronto, but the snow was too bad so I'd decided to stay home," says Lin. "Thirty minutes after I got the phone call from the pound, the sun came out, so I decided to take a slow drive to the Port Perry animal shelter and check out the deaf dog, to see if I could find a home for her." She told herself that she had a better chance of finding a home for the puppy if she'd seen it herself.

The shelter assistant led Lin to the kennels and there lay a tiny, pink-and-white puppy, fast asleep, undisturbed by the roomful of dogs howling and barking around her. "I gently tapped her bed and she jumped up, startled, and then proceeded to greet me as I have never been greeted before," remembers Lin. "That little stubby tail was wagging so hard I thought it would fly off." It was love at first sight.

But what about Ivan? Reason asserted itself and reluctantly Lin put the puppy back. She couldn't disregard his feelings on the matter. "I knew I couldn't take another dog with special needs into the family home without both of us wanting it," she says. "It wouldn't be fair to the dog or to Ivan." She took some Polaroid photos of the puppy. Then she went home to cook Ivan's favourite dinner and persuade him that this puppy needed them.

"It didn't work," Lin reports. "I couldn't say anything to convince him we should have this little dog." She tried appealing to his compassion, reminding him that Brytni and Crumpet wouldn't be around much longer. Finally she told him that if a home wasn't found for this deaf pup in 10 days, it would be killed. Even that was futile. "Nothing," she says, "would convince him to change his mind."

The next week Lin spent every spare second on the phone, trying without success to locate a home for the puppy,. Again and again, people told her to do the dog a favour and put it out of its misery. "All I could think of was that the puppy didn't look like she was miserable at all," says Lin. "In fact, she actually seemed to have an amazing zest for life. Allowing this dog to be euthanized for being deaf seemed so very wrong!"

But there was nothing more she could do. First thing Monday morning the puppy would join the other unadoptable animals slated for the final injection. Lin dragged herself to work that weekend, angry, defeated, and sad. When she came home on Saturday evening, Crumpet and Brytni greeted her as usual. She knelt to hug them, holding back tears. She heard Ivan calling to her from the living room, but she ignored him. She had no energy to pretend to be happy. Then he yelled again: "Happy Valentine's Day, Lin!"

"I looked up and there running towards me was my little pink puppy!" says Lin.

Miss Maggie-Mae, as they named her, was also blind in one eye, but like many Australian shepherds, she was highly intelligent and very eager to work. Lin set out to teach her sign language, and before they knew it Maggie responded to over 130 different signs. She became a certified therapy dog and accompanied Lin to hospitals, nursing homes and schools, Brownie and Cub groups.

But Maggie's best friend was Lin and Ivan's foster son, Justin. "We've had several children with disabilities live with us over the years, but none as long as our Justin," says Lin. "'Just-in-Time,' we call him." Lin and Ivan first met Justin and his mother 10 years ago through a volunteer respite group they worked with. Justin was born a perfect little boy, but at three days of age, a botched routine medical procedure left him clinging to life. "He actually died, was revived and was then air-lifted to Sick Children's Hospital in Toronto," says Lin. "He was kept there until he was four-and-a-half months old, and then he went home with his 17-year-old mom." Oxygen deprivation during the baby's brush with death left him with cerebral palsy, blindness, hydrocephalus, and a severe seizure disorder. It was too much for his young mother to cope with on her own.

"We adored this tiny little boy, and said we'd love to take him on the occasional weekend," says Lin. Before long, the occasional weekend became every weekend, and when Justin was three years old he moved in with them permanently.

Justin, whose hearing is perfect, has a special love for Maggie. "Justin and Maggie-Mae work very well together," says Lin. "Justin doesn't speak and Maggie doesn't hear so it is very easy for him to get her to do tricks!" Lin was invited to take Maggie-Mae into Justin's grade one classroom for a demonstration.

Lin thought carefully about how she wanted to present Maggie to the children. Justin was the only child in his class with a disability, but he was fully integrated within the school system and well accepted by his classmates. He couldn't draw pictures himself, but whenever he brought home pictures done by his classmates, Lin noted with interest that all of the drawings of Justin depicted him standing up, even though none of the children had ever seen him out of his wheelchair. It was as if they hadn't noticed his disability. Lin knew that soon these children would begin to see him differently and treat him differently, so she decided to address the issue directly.

Maggie and Lin went to Justin's school, where the dog proceeded to delight the class, reliably responding to all

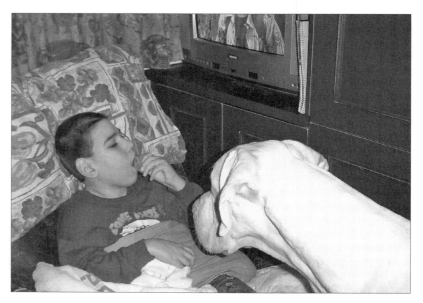

Justin and Nathaniel, a Great Dane

the ASL hand signals she'd learned. The children watched, wide-eyed, while Justin directed the dog to wave and salute, to indicate her age, and to take a bow. Justin, flushed with pride, was the star of the show and Lin's heart swelled to see her boy's hard-won success. It had taken them several years to learn to communicate with Justin. "For 'yes' he bangs his hand down and for 'no' he clasps his hands together," explains Lin. "There was an absolute look of amazement on his face, when he first realized that now he actually had choices in his life." Displaying his skill at communicating with Maggie without using words was a special accomplishment for Justin. Here, finally, was something he could do better than his classmates.

After they were finished, Lin told the children that Maggie was special and asked if anyone knew why. "Justin's buddy threw his hand in the air and announced that Maggie was deaf, and that was why she was special," remembers Lin. She told him he was close but, in fact, what makes each creature special is who they are and what they do, rather than any of their physical attributes. "I pointed out the way Maggie had made them laugh and how good they had felt when they, too, had taken a turn at getting her to do a trick for them!" she says. "It wasn't the actual deafness that had done that, it was Maggie-Mae."

During one of her hospital visits, Lin and Maggie met a small boy and his mother. Lin asked the woman if her son would like to visit with Miss Maggie but the child hid behind his mother and refused to even look at them. His mother apologized, explaining that he was excruciatingly shy and did not speak. He could, however, sign a little. "Perfect!" said Lin. After much nudging and encouragement, the boy indicated he would try getting Maggie to do a trick. "It wasn't more than a few short minutes before he seemingly forgot his shyness and easily managed to get Maggie to take a bow, give a high-five, bark six times to indicate her age, and get a handkerchief out of his pocket when he 'sneezed,'" says Lin. His tearful mother was ecstatic to see her little boy smiling confidently, enjoying his interaction with this unusual hospital visitor.

Lin and Maggie are also regular visitors to the local women's shelter. At one visit, after Maggie did all her tricks, Lin invited the children to ask Maggie questions. The dog would answer; a bark meant "yes" and a paw on Lin's foot meant "no." "The children had some great questions," says Lin. "I translated them into ASL and Maggie gave her answer." Then Lin turned it around on them, asking the children what Maggie was "saying." "They reliably chorused 'yes' or 'no,' as the case may be, and were getting quite excited that they could actually communicate with Maggie," remembers Lin.

When Lin heard about a deaf Great Dane puppy that needed a home, she didn't think twice. This time she had no trouble convincing Ivan. Brytni was old now; Crumpet was already gone. And Justin would be thrilled to have another dog around the house.

Miss Olyvia came to them at seven weeks of age. "Missy, as she is affectionately known, is bi-laterally deaf, blind in her left eye, and has had numerous medical problems," says Lin. But that didn't stop Olyvia for long. To Lin's delight, Maggie took over the raising of this new puppy, firmly teaching her the household rules. "You don't step out of line when Maggie's around," she says. Lin also began teaching American Sign Language to her new pup and, in spite of numerous interruptions for medical crises and operations, Olyvia learned about 40 signs. Lin took Olyvia to a local seniors' centre to socialize her, where she quickly became a favourite. "She's a very special pup that has stolen the hearts of many people," she says.

Around that time, Lin decided Missy needed a companion. Because she knew that deafness is common in the breed, she decided to rescue another Dane that would otherwise be put to sleep. That's when Miss Molly Dukes, who is unilaterally (one ear) deaf, came to them. "It was lovely, seeing the two of them together," says Lin. "Molly weighs 125 pounds and Miss Olyvia is 105."

But then tragedy struck. Maggie, who had barely entered old age, passed away. Lin's first thought, before the grief struck, was, "Who's going to train these puppies?" But Miss Olyvia, a born nurturer, stepped in to take over the role of teacher. Lin was so grateful that they had these two big dogs to comfort them. Justin felt the loss of Maggie keenly, but took great joy in the antics of the Danes.

That's when she got the call about Macy, an all-white, deaf, very unhappy Jack Russell terrier that needed a foster home. "We were her seventh or eighth placement by the time she was 10 months old," says Lin. The little dog was very insecure, poorly socialized, and reacted badly to strangers. Lin jokes, "They blamed her bad disposition on her deafness, but it was really just that she was a Jack Russell terrier." Lin and Ivan decided to try to repair some of the damage and prepare her for a "forever" home.

Macy, like many little dogs, was accustomed to being carried everywhere. And because she couldn't hear, she'd never been allowed to run off-leash. "I took her to a secure park where she could be off-leash and just run," says Lin.

Very quickly Macy learned to keep an eye on Lin at all times. That first run exhausted the little dog, but it didn't take long before her muscle tone increased and she was fit again and ready to try another home.

When the new owners came to pick up Macy, Lin explained carefully about the terrier's exercise requirements and how to handle her behaviour problems ... then crossed her fingers. But the new family didn't listen. In less than a week, Macy was back. "She was just a mess when she returned, and we were right back to where we started with her," says Lin. She knew then that each transition was making her more anxious and less able to bond with another new family. Macy's only "forever" home would be with them.

This meant they had work to do. "What she hates most is being separated from her people, so when she misbehaved, we put her in another room," explains Lin. She could still see them through the glass doors, but she couldn't get to them, a severe punishment for this sensitive dog. Those time-outs taught her quickly.

"Macy, who is much like a running blender with the lid off, is our token small dog," says Lin. "There is not one Dane that doesn't have total respect for Miss Macy. You will often see her standing outside the kitchen door, not allowing anyone else to pass by her, all 13 pounds of her just bristling with indignation." It's not unusual to see the diminutive dog hanging off a Dane jowl in play, to Justin's delight. Miss Macy is Lin's smartest pup and understands about 45 ASL signs.

"She's probably the only one we have that *wants* to do tricks," adds Lin.

A short time later, when Lin was on vacation, she received an e-mail from a friend telling her about three deaf Great Dane puppies that were about to be put down. "I'll save one for you," the friend told her, thinking Lin would be pleased. Lin was relieved to get a second message apologetically telling her the puppies had all been placed already. "Then, when I get off the plane, I'm told 'You're picking up your new dog tomorrow.'" Miss Annie, another bilaterally deaf white Dane, came to them at the age of seven weeks. When she arrived from Toronto she was even smaller than Macy and, from the very beginning, she was a jumper. Fences don't hold her. Gates are a joke. And she's been known to jump *into* open car windows! Today she's a magnificent, massive dog who understands about 30 ASL signs. "Annie is the one to teach bite inhibition to the other dogs," says Lin. They can't hear each other squeal but Annie lets them know when they're playing too hard.

Last, but by no means least, is Nathaniel, who came from a breeder in Michigan. "Each Dane I've taken on has grown successively larger than the one before," says Lin. "Nate is 170 pounds now, 95 cm at the shoulder, and about 18 months old. Like Missy, he's had a rough go with his health. He is bilaterally deaf, blind in his right eye, has had a bone disease, and didn't walk until he was six months old." He's also the most comical dog in Lin's family, regularly sending

Nathaniel

Justin into peals of laughter. In the six months during which he didn't walk, Lin suspects he lounged on his bed dreaming up all the mischief he would get into as soon as he was able.

"That boy can open any door in the house," says Lin. "Yes, he even opens the bathroom doors! We are now diligent about locking them." When he's thirsty, he turns on the tap and gets himself a drink, which would be alright if he'd also turn it off. But what's the point of that?

Nathaniel's favourite trick is to open the garage door and lead all the other dogs across the ramp and into the van. "I have been suckered into driving them to McDonald's on more than one occasion," admits Lin. "After all, who would be able to resist the sight of them all sitting in the van so calmly, just willing me to come along for the ride?" Lin suspects Nathaniel knows about 15 ASL signs, but since he only responds when he wants to, she'll never know for sure.

Much has changed since the Valentine's Day arrival of Miss Maggie-Mae. Justin is now a young teenager, well-accepted at school, where he's treated as normally as possible. "I treasure each and every day we have with him," Lin adds. "Justin is one of God's children and as such, he is as deserving of a life that is every bit as good as anyone else's, despite the challenges he must face on a daily basis." Lin doesn't know what his future holds, but she doesn't fret over it. No one knows what the future holds. All she knows is that potential is made up of far more than physical characteristics.

"To this day I still marvel at the mystical power of my little Miss Maggie-Mae," says Lin. "And to think they all said that Maggie would never amount to anything because *she* was handicapped!"

Chapter 8
From Trash
to Treasure

Hey huddled in the shelter of the doorway, shielding their cigarettes from the wind. Their 15-minute break from the factory routine went all too quickly, and although no one was anxious to return to work, the cold October air and back-alley atmosphere made them glad to butt out and head inside.

But wait. What was that sound coming from the dumpster? They moved closer. Scratching, scuffling noises coming from inside the dumpster weren't unusual. But the sound that made the hair go up at the back of their necks did not come from a rat. It was something else, something most un-animal-like. Something almost like ... a voice.

They ripped away the refuse and debris, clawing their

way through to a sealed cardboard box. They lifted it out. It wasn't heavy, but whatever was inside began shrieking and scratching furiously, unbalancing the flimsy container. The workers yelped and nearly dropped the box. Finally, they got it safely inside. They carefully cut through the tape and opened the flaps. Flattened against the side of the box was a creature just barely recognizable as a bird. But this was a bird like none of them had ever seen before. Scaly black feet clawed at the frigid air and spiky wings flapped clumsily against the cardboard. Bright black eyes blinked with confusion at the sudden light and the strange faces. Beneath the eyes, a large, iron-grey beak opened and snapped shut menacingly. White feathers sprang randomly from a surface of mostly naked, bloodied flesh. It was a Moluccan cockatoo, a beautiful tropical bird wellknown for its intelligence and ability to bond with humans, tossed away like last week's leftovers.

The factory workers immediately called the City of Toronto Animal Control about their unusual find. The City, in turn, contacted Leanne Travis. Leanne, not having seen the bird, figured someone local would take it, but when she learned that after two days without a successful claimant, Animal Control was considering euthanization, she ran down to see what she could do.

"I walked in and saw this big moluccan, real haggard-looking," remembers Leanne. "He was missing feathers, he had ripped into his chest and his tail, he was covered in blood and giant scabs." In spite of his appearance, Leanne's heart went out to him. He must have sensed this, because when she reached for him, he immediately climbed into her arms. She knew then that he was coming home with her. She called him Zane.

For a neglected and abandoned parrot, there's no better place than Leanne's home. She runs Second Flight Parrot Sanctuary, a registered non-profit facility for parrots of all kinds, out of her home in Washago. At the moment she has 17 — she stops to count them all up — from tiny budgies to majestic macaws. Not all of them are permanent residents; if an approved home can be found for a healthy bird, she's happy to place it. But some arrive in such poor condition, or with such severe psychological damage and behavioural problems, that they will never be good companions. These remain with Leanne and her family, to live out their lives in peace and security, surrounded by their own kind.

Leanne had her suspicions about Zane's former owner. "We don't know anything for sure, but a couple of weeks before, we'd receiving repeated, very persistent calls from a man who wanted money for a Moluccan cockatoo he'd inherited," she says. "He kept telling me he'd let me have the bird for only $3000." For a sanctuary with a shoe-string budget, that was out of the question. But the calls, which all originated from the same area code as the factory's, stopped around the time Zane was found. "It's a bit suspicious," Leanne says.

She tries not to be cynical, but it's hard when ignorance

is rampant. Recently she had a telephone request from a man who insisted he wanted a parrot, a big one. "Right off the bat he got my back up," she admits. When she asked him what type of large bird he was interested in, he told her he didn't care, as long as it could talk. Leanne sighed inwardly and explained that many parrots can learn to mimic the human voice, but that there's a wide variety of physical and tempera-mental characteristics among the different species. "I asked him if he'd done any research and he just told me he'd give me a cheque for $2000 if I'd give him a bird right now." Clearly he hadn't done his homework, so Leanne wasn't about to relin-quish any of her birds to his care. She's seen too much dam-age done out of ignorance. "Other organizations might do it," she says, "but not us. You've got to be so careful."

At first Leanne thought Zane would be easy to place. He needed fattening up, of course; he weighed a skeletal 600 grams, instead of the usual 800–850 grams. His damaged flesh was caused by self-mutilation, a common problem among captive birds. Naturally active, social creatures, they are not meant to spend their lives alone in a small cage. Boredom and loneliness is so emotionally damaging to them that they develop the self-destructive habit of feather-plucking, pull-ing out their own feathers the same way we might gnaw our fingernails in times of stress. But the stress for these birds is never-ending and sometimes when the feathers are all gone, they begin picking at the flesh beneath. In Zane's case, he was literally tearing himself apart.

Self-mutilation, like any habit, is a tough problem to break. The first thing was to prevent him from reaching his chest, but this was easier said than done! An Elizabethan collar, commonly used in veterinary hospitals, is a plastic cone-shaped device that fits snugly around the neck, allowing the animal to eat and drink while preventing it from biting or licking at a wound. "We tried using conventional collars, but he figured out how to get everything off," says Leanne. "Then Diane Dwyer, a woman who makes collars specifically for parrots, donated one for him and it worked."

Parrots are experts at hiding any weakness, and after a few days they realized his condition was worse that they'd first thought. Their work with Zane was just beginning. "He was literally a bag of bones. He was obviously a very old bird. He had cataracts and arthritis, and he must have been kept in a very small cage," explains Leanne, "because he could hardly move. His joints were so bad, he couldn't even curl his toes around to hold on to the perches." Leanne knew it would take a lengthy period of extensive rehabilitation for him to recover and even then, it might not be enough. "We didn't know if he was going to make it," Leanne says. "For the first month or so I hardly left his side."

Controlling the feather-picking created another problem. The collar interfered with wing movement, and because birds use their wings in maintaining balance, Zane had even more trouble walking. "I started working with his muscles, getting him to exercise his legs and wings. It took a month or two of physiotherapy," she says, "but once he was able to move around he stopped plucking his feathers. He was able to keep himself busy and enjoy life again. He hasn't picked a day since."

In fact, although he's likely the oldest resident of Second Flight, he's the most active. People who saw him when he first arrived at the sanctuary can hardly believe he's the same bird. "When he came in he was so skinny," says Leanne. "Now I'll ask 'Where's my chunky chicken?' and he responds by fluffing out all his feathers and saying 'Chunky chicken! Chunky chicken!'"

Second Flight has officially been open for two years. Each week about 20 people visit the birds, and the family welcomes them into their home. "We want to educate people about their care and the time they take," Leanne says. The Travis house is large — 3000 square feet — but at the moment, it's not nearly big enough. Birds, cages, perches, and stands cover every surface, in every room. "We're actually running out of space!" says Leanne. "We have a bird room but recently a tree came down on it. By some miracle none of our birds were hurt, although Zane was pretty alarmed. He kept asking 'What'cha doin'? What'cha doin'?'"

Once the bird room, a bright 20 x 30 foot enclosure off the kitchen, is functional again, life may get back to what passes for normal in the Travis household. "All the cockatoos stay in the bird room," Leanne says. "The smaller birds stay in the living room or my bedroom." The macaws and African greys stay in a separate room as well, because they can't tolerate cockatoo feather dust, the chalk-like powder that naturally coats those beautiful white feathers.

Zane was the first bird to put challenging demands on Leanne's time, but not the last. A Goffin cockatoo named Alba arrived in even worse condition than Zane, partially paralyzed and unable to stand or even feed herself. Goffins look similar to Moluccans, but they're smaller, and are prized for their playful, affectionate personalities. Leanne ached to see this gentle creature in such fear and misery. Alba's previous owners had tried to identify and treat her condition but nothing had helped, and there was no apparent cause for her paralysis.

Leanne immediately tucked Alba into an isolation cage in case her condition was infectious. Then came yet another round of medical tests. "She was in quarantine for 45 days," Leanne recalls. "Whenever I spent time with her, I'd change clothes, shower, and wash my hair before I went near any of the other birds." As a result, she spent very little time with Zane during Alba's critical period. But finally, x-rays gave them an answer: Alba had a brain injury. She had been hit — hard.

Instead of letting the anger over this abuse take over, Leanne focused on Alba. She knew that a bird in such dire straits wasn't happy, so she decided to give Alba two, maybe three weeks. If there was no improvement in that time, the right move for the cockatoo would be to consider euthanasia. But Leanne wasn't going to let Alba go without a fight. "For those weeks I was with her 24 hours a day, seven days a week," she remembers. Because of the brain injury her muscles had atrophied, so Leanne began yet another program of physiotherapy. Several times each day, Leanne flexed and extended the bird's limbs, taking them through their full range of motion. Within days, they saw improvement. "She was able to walk again and climb but she was wobbly, a bit like she was drunk," Leanne says. The road to recovery wasn't smooth, but Alba was on her way.

One of Alba's biggest problems was sleeping. Parrots normally sleep while perched, but because of her neurological damage, every time she began to relax she fell off her perch. "We designed a special cage for her," says Leanne. "It had flat perches, a little padded hut, and a blanket at the bottom of the cage. But there were many times she still couldn't sleep. I'd see her sitting and she'd start to tip over. She'd struggle with it, then give a little cry." Leanne couldn't bear to watch her becoming more and more exhausted, so for several nights she sat in an armchair with Alba on her chest, surrounded by pillows. Secure, Alba finally got the rest she needed.

As Alba progressed, Leanne began bringing her down to the parrot room to be with the other birds during the day, but she still kept a close eye on her. Jungle law is pitiless to the injured or sick and natural instinct for most birds dictates that the weak one be killed to protect the strength of the flock. Only one bird seemed to realize this vulnerable bird posed no threat. "Zane was the only one I'd trust with Alba," says Leanne. "He'd go up and sit next to her very quietly, and check her out for awhile, and then he'd preen her. After a few minutes he'd have had enough and would walk away."

Then one day, Alba decided to let Leanne know she was feeling much better. Like many of the birds at Second Flight, Alba quickly learned to call Leanne "Mom" — the only word she spoke. "I was bathing a macaw in the bathroom and I heard this little voice say, 'Mom?' Alba had climbed out of her cage and walked all the way out of my room to the bathroom," says Leanne. It was a formidable journey for a bird with such significant mobility problems.

For about six months Alba improved slowly but steadily. "Then one day she was on the floor," says Leanne, "and I just thought something didn't look right." Leanne made an appointment to take Alba to the animal hospital but within five minutes of the time Leanne hung up the telephone, Alba went into a seizure. While the unconscious bird twitched and thrashed, Leanne wrapped her in soft towels and rushed her to the hospital. After an hour of seizing — a horrific insult to the body — Alba finally stopped, only to begin again moments later. Even heavy medication couldn't quell the attack. While Leanne stood by helplessly, Alba, the little bird that wouldn't give up, died.

Leanne was overwhelmed with frustration and grief. "For two days I was a wreck," she remembers. But there are always other birds to help, and other people to educate. And there's always her human family, too. "My husband is extremely supportive," she says. "I once got a call about a bird in Montreal and I was trying to figure out what to do. It's a long drive. But my husband immediately said, 'Let's go!'" Their five children consider the birds part of the family, too, and have learned to be expert parrot handlers. Leanne didn't realize just how much they'd learned until nine-year old Michayla came into the kitchen one day with blood pouring down her arm and Kiko, an unpredictable citron cockatoo, hanging off her arm by his beak. Kiko had been aggressive when he arrived but had learned to trust both Leanne and Michayla. This time, however, he'd been startled by another bird while Michayla was playing with him. "She came up to me and said, 'Mom, you know how you taught me not to react when they bite? Can you get him off me so I can go upstairs and react?'"

Such incidents aren't unusual with parrots; besides flight, their main method of defence is their powerful beaks. Once they've learned that humans can be dangerous, it is difficult to regain their trust. That's partly why Zane is so unusual. Whatever the circumstances of his former life, it has not taken away his love for people, especially children. "We take him to the park in a harness and if he sees kids he runs over to give them kisses," says Leanne. But it is his compassion for the new birds, the frightened, the lost, or the sick that gives him the reputation as a one-bird welcoming committee. "He'll come over to check them out, and then he'll sit there and talk to them," says Leanne.

There's only one bird Zane doesn't get along with: Elmo, another moluccan cockatoo. This bird, Leanne explains, was very aggressive when he arrived. She still has the scar where he broke her finger. Over time he mellowed, but now and then he gets up to his old tricks. "One time he decided to sneak up behind me," says Leanne. "I knew he was there but I wanted to see what he'd do. Sure enough, he tried to ambush me. But before he could, Zane flew in, fluffed out his feathers, and chased Elmo back to his cage. Then he sat there making his special 'I protected you, Mom!' sounds." For the rest of the day Zane kept a close eye on Elmo, refusing to give him a second chance to attack Leanne. "It's not jealousy, because he lets me give attention to the other birds," emphasizes Leanne. "Zane is just trying to protect me."

It's hard work, and money is always an issue. Leanne estimates that the sanctuary brings in about $1000 each month. Expenses, however, are usually about $2500–3000 each month. Although they build a lot of their own bird toys and their food is generously donated by the Hagen pet food company, there are always new cages to buy and, of course, the expense of travelling to pick up yet another bird. But Leanne has big dreams for the future. She'd like to build a free-standing facility, just for the birds. She'd like to have an isolation ward to quarantine sick birds, a giant aviary, and maybe even a veterinarian on site.

It seems a far cry from reality, as she goes about the daily tasks of cleaning cages, chopping vegetables, and answering phone calls, but she doesn't let the mundane work get her down. She reminds herself of how Zane looked when he first arrived and compares that ragged specimen to the vibrant bird he is today. She remembers Alba's courage, and her little voice saying, "Mom?" Despite all they've been through, these birds keep fighting. No matter how they've been hurt, they stay sweet. That's what keeps Leanne working; that's what feeds her dreams.

Chapter 9
Marilyn the DoberMom

hen she arrived at the Kitchener-Waterloo Humane Society shelter in March of 2002, facility workers eyed her with care. She had the tall, strong build typical of her breed. But instead of exuding an air of power, this stray Doberman cowered when they reached for her — a potentially dangerous sign. Would she turn on them? Even if she wasn't mean, fear could make her desperate enough to react with violence. Her sunken eyes and protruding ribs gave evidence of a life filled with deprivation and sadness. If she'd never known kindness, could she be trusted?

Warily, they led her to a kennel where she would at least be warm, dry, and fed until someone came to claim her. But when the other dogs greeted her with a deafening chorus of howls and yelps, she recoiled in terror.

Shelter workers soon realized no one was coming to claim Marilyn, as they'd begun calling her. Nor was she dangerous; she was simply terrified of everything around her. "She was very skittish and clingy," says Mark Womack of the Kitchener-Waterloo Humane Society. She'd apparently never learned to trust people or explore new places. They estimated she was about three years old and, because she'd obviously just weaned a litter of puppies, shelter workers speculated she was a breeding dog, perhaps in a puppy mill. Her future looked bleak. A mature dog, poorly socialized and badly neglected, she had little chance of finding a good home.

But they did what they could. They began letting Marilyn out of her cage so she could be near them. "We put her in our kitchen where we prepare the animals' food," explains Mark. If she spent more time with people, they reasoned, and had the chance to meet shelter volunteers and visitors, hopefully she'd relax and become more confident.

Around that time a litter of kittens was brought in. When the big dog heard the newborn orphans mewing, she became very agitated. She hovered at the doorway, as close to them as possible, whining and crying. After they'd finished bottle-feeding the babies they brought one of them over to Marilyn. "She warmed up to it immediately," Mark says, "licking it, and letting it crawl all over her." Her fears and anxieties disappeared in her efforts to mother this motherless creature. When they introduced the rest of the litter to her, she sniffed them all thoroughly, lay down beside them, and stretched out on her side. The kittens happily snuggled in, nudging tenaciously against her thin flanks. Even though she had no milk left, Marilyn willingly allowed them to suckle. The shelter workers were somewhat taken aback by her insistence on nurturing this litter, but could see no harm in it, since both she and the kittens were clearly getting what they needed from each other. "She ended up adopting the entire litter," says Mark. The little family became inseparable, and eventually the humane society gave them their own private "maternity ward."

Marilyn quickly became a local media sweetheart. Soon, radio stations all across North America had picked up the story. By the time her kittens were old enough to go to their new homes, "Marilyn the DoberMom" was famous. Over 300 people, from as far away as Halifax and Kentucky, applied to adopt her. How would they decide which home was best for her? Despite the confidence she displayed with the kittens, Marilyn was still a vulnerable dog that needed special care from experienced dog owners.

When the adoption committee read through all the applications, a couple from Sault Ste. Marie stood out. Peggy and Ron Lund had owned Dobermans since the late '70s, and they lived on a large, private, semi-rural property, perfect for this active breed. Their third Doberman, Dallas, had recently succumbed to cancer at the age of five. Although they'd purchased their first two dogs as puppies, straight from reputable breeders, Dallas had come to them as a rescue. Now that he was gone, they wanted to rescue another needy Doberman.

Often, by the time a cute Doberman puppy grows into a strong and wilful destruction-machine, its frustrated owners have had enough. It's not uncommon, say the Lunds, for Dobermans to show up at shelters and rescue facilities at around one year of age, untrained and out-of-control, but otherwise fine. "People often get a Doberman without knowing their energy requirements," says Peggy. "They can be a handful." With proper training, a firm hand, and lots and lots of exercise, many of these dogs can become wonderful pets. And Marilyn had shown that they can have a gentle, maternal temperament.

Her motherly ways had leaped to the Lund's minds when they first saw the Humane Society's ad, and they immediately thought about Malcolm. A few years earlier, after their yard had been dug up for some repair work, their Doberman, Dallas, had found a screaming, badly wounded juvenile black squirrel. "His tree had been disrupted by the landscape work and we think he fell out of the nest," says Peggy. He was in tremendous pain from a broken hind leg. Ron wrapped him up and drove to the animal hospital. After much consideration, and four hospital visits, they decided to have the leg surgically repaired. By the time the leg was healed, the squirrel had become part of the family. They named him Malcolm and now he lives with them in the house. "I never realized how personable a squirrel could be," says Ron. "He runs up my leg and sits on my shoulder. He knows his name, too. When we call him, he jumps out and comes to the cage door to see what we want."

"So when we saw Marilyn on TV," says Peggy, "we thought, 'look how she's treating those kittens! She'd be great with Malcolm!'" Ron knew there would be a great deal of interest in such a dog and their chances would be slim. But they sent in an application anyway. "When we applied to adopt her, we were asked for a veterinary reference," says Ron. "Our vet told them, 'They're such animal lovers they even had me pin a broken leg on a squirrel.'" As soon as the committee heard about Malcolm, their decision was unanimous: Marilyn would go to the Lunds. When Ron and Peggy went to pick her up, the cameras were snapping as journalists reported her happy ending. "It's kind of neat," says Ron. "Our Doberman, Dallas, found Malcolm, and Malcolm helped us get Marilyn."

On the drive home from Kitchener-Waterloo, they stopped at a drive-through to buy Marilyn a celebratory treat: her own burger. But after a half-hearted sniff, Marilyn turned up her nose at it. "She's the only Doberman we've ever had who was uninterested in a hamburger," says Peggy. "I believe it showed how unsocialized she really was. No one had ever given her a piece of hamburger and she didn't know how good it might be." This, they vowed, would change.

But Marilyn's adventures weren't over yet. "The first day we got home, we took Marilyn for a nice long walk," says Ron. After the walk he took off her leash and let her onto the deck so she could watch him feed the wild squirrels. But the minute he turned his back, he heard a thump. Marilyn had leaped over the edge of the deck and hared off down the driveway, oblivious to Ron's frantic calls.

Ron and Peggy hopped into the car and drove to the road. There they flagged down passing motorists to ask if they'd seen a big black dog. No one had. Marilyn had disappeared into the thick bush. "We had a whole search party out looking for her," recalls Peggy. "But although we called and called, searched and searched, we covered miles without a single sighting." Peggy worried that Marilyn was trying to run back to her kittens in Kitchener, an eight hour drive away. As the daylight ebbed, they felt worse and worse. The weather report predicted snow that night, and Marilyn's short coat wouldn't provide sufficient protection. "What really bothered us was that these people took a long time to decide on the best home for her, and we felt we'd let them all down," says Ron. "Less than 12 hours after we'd gotten her, she'd disappeared. But, as timid as she was, who'd have expected her to jump the fence?"

Finally, they had to admit defeat. "We needed a village," says Peggy. "We couldn't find her ourselves." They swallowed their pride, phoned the local radio station, and asked them to let the public know that Marilyn the DoberMom was lost! Peggy and Ron knew that it wouldn't be long until the people at Kitchener-Waterloo's Humane Society found out what happened and they braced themselves for criticism.

But that's not what happened. "People called and even came out from Sault Ste. Marie to help look for her," says

Peggy. Everyone wanted to find Marilyn. "One neighbour," says Ron, "offered his brand new four-wheeler to look in the bush." They'd never met him before.

A long, cold night passed with no success. The next morning, as Ron wondered what they were going to do, he looked out the window and something caught his eye. His heart leaped: it was a black-and-tan body moving about in the trees. "We were so worried she was lost somewhere in the bush. But wow!" he says. "She was still around!" Marilyn, however, wouldn't come to them. It was frustrating, but understandable. "She didn't know us," says Peggy. "She didn't know the area. We didn't even know if she would respond to her name. 'Marilyn' was just what they'd called her at the humane society."

That's when Ron had an idea. "We decided to get hold of a kitten," he says. "We knew that somehow the kittens did something for her, so we thought it was worth a try." Many phone calls later, they'd located a humane society nearby that had a five-week old kitten they were willing to lend them, but only temporarily. The woman who was attempting to nurse the kitten back to health told them, "This kitten may not live long but if, in its short life, it can help you get your dog back, it's accomplished something worthwhile."

When the kitten arrived, Peggy cradled it in her hands and walked outside. They waited. The kitten didn't make a sound. There was no movement from the bushes. "Here we'd been told this kitten cried all the time," says Peggy, "but at the critical moment it didn't make a peep!" For the rest of the day,

Ron and Peggy carried the kitten from one Marilyn sighting to another, over five square kilomtres of bush, without success.

Nightfall approached again and they looked at each other in despair. Another day of failure. Then, in the adjoining field, they saw a shadow. Could it be Marilyn? With guarded hope, Peggy grabbed the kitten's kennel and ran out for one last try. She picked up the kitten and held it towards the shadow. This time, the furry mite gave a little squeak. Within seconds, Peggy spotted Marilyn through the trees, inching her way towards them. Her heart leaped but she willed herself to stay calm. "If I'd called her, she wouldn't have come. But she came for the kitten," she adds. "She just couldn't resist that piteous mewing."

Finally Marilyn got within arm's reach. Peggy reached over and casually took hold of her collar, but the big dog didn't even notice; she was busy nuzzling the baby. "I cannot put into words the relief I felt when I grasped Marilyn's collar!" says Peggy. "Tears literally flowed down my cheeks."

When it was time for the kitten to go back the Lunds watched Marilyn anxiously. How would she react to having "her" baby taken away? They'd never wanted a cat, fearing for the squirrels that visited the feeders in the yard — not to mention Malcolm — but perhaps, for Marilyn's sake, they should keep this one. As it turned out, that wasn't an option. Because of the kitten's delicate health, she required a great deal of care. The woman fostering it had already bonded with it, and decided to keep it.

After some initial sniffing and whining, Marilyn accepted the disappearance of this latest baby. Peggy and Ron kept a close eye on her, willing to do anything to help her feel like part of the family. "All our other Dobes slept on the bed with us," says Ron. "When we first got Marilyn, Peggy said, 'Nope, no bad habits this time.' But once we got her back, we let her up on the bed, and that was it. Eventually she bonded with us."

Peggy and Ron initially thought they'd change her name. After all, Marilyn is an unlikely name for a dog. But she was a local celebrity. "We'd have people stop us on the street to ask us about her," says Peggy. "They'd say, 'Is that Marilyn? I'm so glad you found her!' So we decided to leave it."

The name may have been settled, but the cat issue wasn't. They still worried that Marilyn was lonely, but they couldn't have anything that would jeopardize Malcolm or his wild cousins. Then Ron noticed a feral cat lurking beneath their deck. Naturally, he started leaving out food for it. It was extremely wary of humans and wouldn't leave the safety of its hideout until Ron had gone back inside the house. "This was one tough cat," he says. "I saw him chase a fox away from his food one day." Eventually the cat would eat while Ron was still outside. And his patience paid off. "Finally," he says, "I lured it inside." He wanted to find it a good home. Once reassured that he could trust this family, the cat revealed his loving nature. Ron took it to the veterinarian to be vaccinated and neutered, thinking it would be easier to find him a good home if all those details were already taken care of. But a

Marilyn

surprise awaited them. "They discovered he was diabetic," Ron says wryly. "So we had to keep him. Who wants a cat that needs a needle every day? But he's turned into an awesome pet." Because of his sleek, black fur, they named him Merlin.

"Malcolm, Marilyn, and Merlin," says Peggy. "*We* liked the sound of it, but Marilyn was getting confused, so mostly we call the cat Kitty."

Marilyn and Merlin hit it off immediately and, to their relief, the cat has no interest in Malcolm. Perhaps he remembers his days of homelessness and hunger. Perhaps Marilyn has convinced him to stay. Whatever the reason, this cat doesn't want to go outside anymore. "If you open the door, he runs the other way," says Ron. "He knows he's found a good thing and he's not leaving."

In the Lund's queen-sized bed Ron and Peggy fight for space. The cat purrs happily on one side; the dog yawns and stretches her long frame out on the other. There is barely any similarity between the regal Marilyn of today and the cowering, nameless dog that had arrived at the shelter two years earlier. "Marilyn has turned into such a confident dog," says Peggy. "She's happy to visit with other dogs. She likes to meet new people. And she looks proud; she holds her head high."

She has plenty of reason to be proud. This unglamourous, untrained, unsocialized dog has turned into a princess, a diva, a heart-stealer. "We couldn't love her more," says Ron. "We've had three Dobermans before her, and they were all great dogs, but they were nothing like Marilyn."

Recently, Marilyn was awarded the Ontario SPCA Animal of the Year Award. Not only did she help change attitudes towards Dobermans and shelter animals in general.

She also helped five kittens get a good start on life, and convinced Peggy and Ron Lund to keep Merlin. "You don't have to get a dog from a breeder," Peggy reflects. "You can save a dog that's unwanted for whatever reason. 'Throw-away dogs' can be equal to or better than any other dogs."

Epilogue

Wherever Matthew goes these days, Cooper, his guardian and friend, goes too. And each day, the bond between them grows stronger.

Matthew's parents do everything they can to keep them together, but sometimes it's not possible. When Trish noticed a lump on Cooper's hind leg, she knew this meant a trip to the animal hospital. Matthew would insist on coming along, but he had a morbid fear of medical procedures. "He claims he can remember every needle he ever had after he was born," says Trish. In the days before Cooper, it took three adults to hold Matthew down to have a blood sample drawn. Now, he's able to handle it without being restrained. But how would he react if Cooper needed treatment?

At the animal hospital, the veterinarian examined the lump. She was concerned it might be a tumour, and explained that she needed to extract a tiny sample of cells from the mass — with a needle. Matthew watched her suspiciously while she talked, but managed to contain his anxiety. When the doctor removed the cap from the needle and took Cooper's paw in her hand, however, Matthew panicked. He leaped up and threw himself between her and Cooper, determined to prevent anyone from hurting his beloved pal. "It took both me and my husband to restrain him," says Trish, "but after sensing that his Coopey wasn't hurt, he calmed down." The biopsy indicated that the mass was cancer, but with surgical removal Cooper could expect a full recovery.

Cooper's surgery went well. He spent six weeks resting and healing, with Matthew watching over him as much as possible. No one was happier than Matthew when Cooper was finally able to get back to work again.

Cooper came into Matthew's life to be a safety aid, but he's become something much more important. In a million tiny ways he increases Matthew's ability to cope with life, helping him face events that threaten to overwhelm him, and encouraging him when he's anxious. When Matthew gets that look on his face that means he's headed for a melt-down, Cooper stands close by, nudging him softly with his muzzle. Sometimes he puts his head in Matthew's lap. Matthew pauses, leans against the firm, warm body, and runs his fingers through the silky fur. In a matter of moments, his anxiety and frustration begin to dissipate. The tension leaves his muscles. The expression on his face becomes peaceful. His overwhelming world becomes manageable again. All because of a big dog that loves him.

Web Sites

To learn more about service dogs, visit National Service Dogs at: www.nsd.on.ca/ or Pacific Assistance Dogs at: padsdogs. org/

To learn more about the Ontario SPCA, visit them at: www.ospca.on.ca/

To learn more about miniature donkeys, visit the Donkey Sanctuary of Canada at: www.donkeysanctuary.ca/

To learn more about parrot rescue, visit Second Flight Parrot Sanctuary at: www.secondflight.org/

Acknowledgments

My sincere thanks to the many people who so generously shared their experiences with me for this book: Dave Guest, Jenni Rowe-Matheis, Pat and Joe Bergeron, Rose Kimber, Nancy Ambrogio, Tim and Trish Brown, Sandy Pady, Karen Pollard, Morgan Jarvis, Lin Gardinor, Leanne Travis, Mark Womack, and Ron and Peggy Lund.

I'm also grateful to my skilled editor, Deborah Lawson, for gently but firmly smoothing out the rough spots.

About the Author

Roxanne Willems Snopek lives in Abbotsford, British Columbia, with her family and assorted animals. Her award-winning articles and essays have appeared in a variety of publications, including *The Vancouver Sun*, *Woman's World*, *Reader's Digest*, and multitudes of pet periodicals. This is her fourth book for Altitude Publishing and she has more in the works. As well, she is writing a mystery series set in the veterinary world. In her spare time she practises agility with her poodle, Myshkin, who is far better at it than she is.

Photo Credits

Cover: ROB & SAS/CORBIS; Tim and Trish Brown: page 67; Peter Buss: page 42; Lin Gardinor: pages 96, 102; David Guest: page 18; Ronald and Peggy Lund: page 125; Roxanne Willems Snopek: page 132.

Amazing Author Question and Answer

What was your inspiration for writing about this topic?

The idea came after I wrote my first book, *Great Dog Stories*. There are many animal heroes other than dogs, but they aren't as well known. I wanted to write about some of these.

What surprised you most while you were researching the topic?

I had no idea donkeys are such comedic characters, or that they are used as guard animals!

What escapade do you most identify with?

I've worked with parrots before, so my memory was jolted by the story of Leanne Travis's daughter, Michayla, who came to Leanne with a parrot hanging off her arm. While I've never been badly bitten, I have great respect for those powerful beaks. Parrots are fascinating creatures, but they need far more than most people can give them. I'm glad people like Leanne are there to pick up the pieces!

What difficulties did you run into when researching this topic?

I thought I'd be writing about dogs pulling people from burning buildings and other obviously heroic behaviour. What I discovered, unfortunately, is that most animal heroism stems from their courage in overcoming the cruelty or neglect inflicted upon them by people.

Why did you become a writer? Who inspired you?

I've loved both animals and books for as long as I can remember. Reading about animals was always a favourite pastime, and writing about animals is a natural progression for me. I studied to become a registered veterinary technician and enjoyed the work, but I always had this idea that one day I'd write a book. It wasn't until I left veterinary practice to raise my children that I began writing seriously. After a decade of writing for magazines and newspapers, I took the plunge into writing books. And here I am, with my fourth published book, *Inspiring Animal Tales.*

What part of the writing process do you enjoy most?

The best part of writing an Amazing Story is researching the possibilities and talking with other animal lovers. When I hear a great anecdote, something clicks in my brain. It's an *ah-ha!* moment, because I know I've just heard a great story my readers will love! And I always enjoy learning new things about animals and our relationship with them.

Who are your Canadian heroes?

I have many Canadian heroes, but three of them are: Rene Chartrand, because of the way he cares for the cats of Parliament Hill; Carol Shields, for writing *The Stone Diaries*; and all the people at National Service Dogs, for training those animals so magnificently.

What is your next project?

I'm working on a fictional mystery series set in the veterinary world, based on the human-animal bond. The first one, entitled *Targets of Affection*, will be released in 2006 by Cormorant Books. It deals with the link between animal abuse and child abuse.

Which other Amazing Stories would you recommend?

As a murder mystery fan, I've enjoyed Susan McNicoll's *British Columbia Murders* and *Ontario Murders*. And for everyone who's read and reread Anne of Green Gables, I recommend Stan Sauerwein's biography, *Lucy Maud Montgomery*.

by the same author!

AMAZING STORIES™

GREAT DOG STORIES

Inspirational Tales About
Exceptional Dogs

ANIMAL/HUMAN INTEREST
by Roxanne Willems Snopek

GREAT DOG STORIES
Inspirational Tales About
Exceptional Dogs

*"His name is not wild dog anymore, but the
first friend, because he will be our friend for
always and always and always."*
Rudyard Kipling

Dogs have long acted as protectors, but they are
also an inspiration to many people who work
closely with them. From seeing-eye dogs to tracking dogs, the bond formed with canine companions can be exceptionally rewarding. The author
features the stories of nine incredible dogs and
their owners.

 True stories. Truly Canadian.

ISBN 1-55153-946-2

AMAZING STORIES™

GREAT CAT STORIES

Incredible Tales About
Exceptional Cats

ANIMAL/HUMAN INTEREST

by Roxanne Willems Snopek

GREAT CAT STORIES
Incredible Tales About
Exceptional Cats

*"There are many intelligent species in the
universe. They are all owned by cats."*
Anonymous

The bond between cat and human is a powerful
thing. Those who have shared their lives with a cat
have experienced first-hand the enchanting spell
cast by our feline friends. From strays that slink
their way into the homes and hearts of unsus-
pecting individuals, to pampered purebreds that
rule the household, cats have a tendency to make
themselves indispensable to their human companions. This is a collection of stories about special cats and the people who love them.

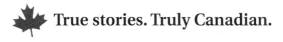 True stories. Truly Canadian.

ISBN 1-55153-777-X

TRUE CANADIAN
AMAZING STORIES™

WILDLIFE IN THE KITCHEN

...And Other Great Animal Tales

WILDLIFE/HUMAN INTEREST

by Roxanne Willems Snopek

WILDLIFE IN THE KITCHEN
...And Other Great Animal Tales

"She lavishes tenderness on all the patients that come through her door, but her mission is clear: to rehabilitate them and send them back to their natural environment."

Every year, thousands of wild animals across Canada are injured or orphaned. While many perish in the harsh conditions of their natural habitat, some survive and thrive thanks to the compassionate individuals who rescue and rehabilitate our nation's wildlife. From caring for baby birds and raccoons to ensuring the safety of beluga whales and polar bears, these special Canadians have opened their hearts — and sometimes their homes — to animals in need. Here are some of their heartwarming stories.

 True stories. Truly Canadian.

ISBN 1-55439-008-7

AMAZING STORIES™

THE HEART OF A HORSE

Poignant Tales and Humorous Escapades

ANIMAL/HUMAN INTEREST

by Gayle Bunney

THE HEART OF A HORSE
Poignant Tales and Humorous Escapades

*"With the first jump, I would be trying to
bring that old pony's head up and around
to stop him. By the second jump, I was
already looking for the perfect place to land.
By the third jump I had mentally said my
'Goodbye Cruel World' speech. By the fourth I
was picking dirt out from between my teeth."*

This collection of heart-warming tales of one
woman's passion for horses covers the spectrum from breeding and training, to adventures
involving grizzly bears, uncooperative cows, and
a truck named Herman. Gayle Bunney's comic
insights bring to life the wild and wonderful
experience of living with horses.

 True stories. Truly Canadian.

ISBN 1-55153-994-2

OTHER AMAZING STORIES

These titles are available wherever you buy books. If you have trouble finding the book you want, call the Altitude order desk at **1-800-957-6888**, e-mail your request to: **orderdesk@altitudepublishing.com** or visit our Web site at **www.amazingstories.ca**

New AMAZING STORIES titles are published every month.